I Didn't Sign Up
For This!

I Didn't Sign Up For This!

*7 Strategies for Dealing With Difficulty
in Difficult Times*

Sandra A. Crowe MA, PCC

Two Harbors Press

Minneapolis, MN

Two Harbors Press
212 3rd Avenue North, Suite 290
· Minneapolis, MN 55401
612.455.2293
www.TwoHarborsPress.com

ISBN-13: 978-1-937928-24-7
LCCN: 2012932910

Distributed by Itasca Books

Cover Design and Typeset by Sophie Chi

Printed in the United States of America

Author Contact Information
Email: sc@pivpoint.com
www.SandraCrowe.com
Facebook: Facebook.com/SandraSpeaks4u
Twitter: @SandraSpeaks4U
Linked In: Linkedin.com/in/SandraCrowe

Contents

Introduction .... *vii*

Chapter 1: 1
Face Down in the Dirt, Looking Up

Chapter 2: 15
What Were You Expecting?

Chapter 3: 25
Helicopter Perspective
   Strategy #1: Assess Reality

Chapter 4: 31
What Hit You Could Not Have Missed You
   Strategy #2: Accept Reality

Chapter 5: 39
Finally Feeling
   *Strategy #3: Fully Feeling Starts Fully
   Healing*

Chapter 6: 45

The Thinking That Got You In Won't Get You Out.

Strategy #4: Redirect Your Thinking

Chapter 7: 55

Difficult Interactions with Self

Strategy #5: Interact with YOU Differently

Chapter 8: 77

Difficult Interactions with Others

Strategy #6: Change the Conversation

Chapter 9: 113

Sandpaper for the Soul

Strategy #7: Glean the Lesson

Chapter 10: 123

Lesson Revealed: A Meal for the Beloved

Appendix *131*

Acknowledgments *133*

Introduction

Dearest Reader,

As a coach, speaker, and author for the past twenty-some odd years, I'm used to helping other people solve their problems. The questions we examine together and the places we go in conversation help managers, organizations, and individuals elicit deep healing. I thought I really knew how to get to the core of organizational and personal issues. But just when I thought I'd learned everything there was to learn in my line of work, the floor opened up and revealed "the more." I had an experience so profoundly terrifying, revealing, and debilitating that it opened me up to not only a new level of being with myself, but to a new world of possibility for my clients and those I serve. This book is the result of that experience.

I sit here, eight years later, the details of my journey still readily available, but the memory of it more dreamlike. I am finally ready to share some of the secrets for dealing with difficulty, for uncovering healing—the real healing—and for revealing its hidden jewels.

Most self-help books are focused on your outer circumstances—financial success in fourteen days, lose twenty pounds in ten hours, etc. In this book, we're talking about how to heal internally, no matter what is happening externally. You will learn how to move through thoughts that cease to race, how to heal deep pain in your heart, and look at yourself in the face of difficult interactions. Before we landscape the outside, we have to clean house.

On the following pages you'll find personal journal writings, lessons learned, methodologies used, and insights about the polished jewel that can emerge within from all difficult experiences. The solutions are as much in the methodologies as they are in the lessons.

Part of the challenge in healthy functioning for any of us is to merge and monitor the thoughts of the mind with the feelings of the heart and let each of them have a say. Interestingly enough, this goes hand in hand with research from the Institute of HeartMath, a nonprofit organization dedicated to the science of the heart and its associated functions. Consider the following:

We have now learned that communication between the heart and brain is actually a dynamic, ongoing, two-way dialogue, with each organ continuously influencing the other's function. Research has shown that the heart communicates to the brain in four major ways: neurologically (through the transmission of nerve impulses), biochemically (via hormones and neurotransmitters), biophysically (through pressure waves), and energetically (through electromagnetic field interactions). Communication along all these conduits significantly affects the brain's activity. Moreover, our research shows that messages the heart sends the brain can also affect performance.

While we may try to separate the heart and the brain, research tells us that they are inseparable. So I've taken that which we know and that which I have experienced and brought the two together.

At its essence, this book is about awareness—awareness of not only the subtle layer of challenge, but its flavors and, most importantly, what it reveals to us.

Gleaning the lesson is what transforms us into the diamond. Otherwise, we are just having experiences. The key to full living—and if you need it, complete healing—is to find the pain, feel it, and allow its existence to be inside you, and bring Divine qualities to transform it into something else, something inherently beneficial. The challenge in this is to be so fully in the feeling that resistance, inner conversations, and outer distractions don't get in your way. If you can truly find that feeling, allow it, and even surrender to it, then the opportunity to leave it arises. But to get to this place, you must be aware of what it is you want to move through you—what feeling, what belief, what way of thinking has taken home within you that is no longer welcome. This book will help you do that.

I believe that the experiences we have are the Divine's way of getting our attention, showing us where to focus and where to take our lessons, so that who we truly are can shine. If you accept that premise, or even part of it, then the energy you need for plowing through, for taking the necessary steps and learning the lessons, will arise; and you will be able to do the necessary work. My deepest wish is that this understanding, these thoughts, and ultimately these solutions serve you at the highest and most profound levels.

Many Blessings,
Sandra A. Crowe
September 8, 2011

Chapter 1

Face Down in the Dirt, Looking Up

Each gain in life represents the loss of something else. We simply never move forward without losing something.
—Catherine Woodward Thomas

January 6, 2004
It's 2:13 p.m. on a cold, wet January afternoon and I am consumed with the thought of air. Fresh air. I want to breathe it, envelop and devour it. For my freedom is contained within its undefined borders. At this moment, it is all that exists for me.

October 26, 2003, was supposed to be an exciting day. Moving day. Stressful, it was nonetheless an opportunity for new surroundings, people and, yes, even a new life. The latter I got in spades.

The day had been especially stressful, the movers in a hurry to get to their next job (and unbeknown to me, licking their chops over my personal belongings), and me in a hurry to organize things for a busy week. Moving was a check on a long list of things to do.

At the end of that long day, and after dealing with movers stealing cash, credit cards, and some of my things, I generously threw my body into bed, grateful for its acceptance. I was so tired that I didn't even notice the new carpet smells or fresh oil paint laid earlier that day. But they noticed me.

After a half hour of barely dosing, I awoke to a stench I could not bear. The closed doors had trapped the toxic smells. I couldn't breathe. My eyes opened in panic and I got up and raced out of the house, going back to my old place to spend the night.

I spent most of that night shaking, throwing up, and feeling as if somebody had been holding a gun to my head. The panic that ran through my body was relentless. It held me prisoner and, when I begged for mercy, I felt as if it laughed. I was trapped in an inner and outer world I thought only existed on paper. It was an unfamiliar torture whose origin I couldn't place and, from where I was held, couldn't be seen. That night initiated a bizarre kind of paralysis which was nearly impossible to explain.

Almost three months later, I have become the bubble girl. Able to go almost nowhere, I am trapped in a world with complete boundary. One by one my friends' houses have become intolerable and I have become more sensitive. My sense of smell and constant endless shaking have become acute and profound. Simply washing my hair is an ordeal, as the tiniest odors are overwhelming, and the body trembles are so severe they block movement. I can smell a newspaper from across the room. If someone down the street is painting his or her house, my nose knows. Cologne is identifiable way before a person arrives and long after his or her disappearance.

Brain fog, or not being able to think clearly, is a way of life. Now, just remembering the keys would be easy. I can't remember my name sometimes, stumbling over words while confusion sets in. It's like living in a tunnel, only there's no light awaiting, no place to go. I am going around in circles, day in and day out.

Last night, while staying at another friend's house, I got a new air filter, thinking that would bring some relief. After shaking uncontrollably until 5:30 a.m., I finally got up and left the room. I went downstairs and lay on the sofa, continuing to shake while my most core inner fears presented themselves.

"When will this end?" "How will I survive?" "What do I do?" Perhaps in any other state these questions might be ordinary concerns; but from here, from this place of profound terror, they feel like questions that hold me to a thread of life, a thread that feels like it's slipping through.

Growth Experience Noted

That was from a journal entry in January of 2004, approximately three months after discovering I had sustained something labeled a "chemical injury" after moving into a new house. You may have heard about "sick building syndrome," environmental illness, or chemical allergies; they are all synonyms for the same thing. Basically, everything you smell, come into contact with, or potentially ingest makes you sick…very sick. Many people don't recover or end up living in the woods, becoming homeless, and in some way retreating from life. In my case, I was homeless temporarily, lived in my car, outside, in other people's houses, and was not able to go into a restaurant, movie theater, mall, social gathering, or any other "normal" event for more than a year. And that yearlong period was the end of the beginning. I continued to recover for another five years after that. The fight to stay in the world was the way I learned how to heal and be healed.

I often call myself God's guinea pig. Nine years prior to the chemical injury, I was living with chronic pain as the result of a number of car accidents I'd had. As a professional consultant, I was helping others deal with difficult situations, but I was in search of ways to help myself. My entire identity had become infused with the pain in my body—a body that was unresponsive to medical treatment and could only be numbed by painkillers.

My realization that I had to find my way—not just back to good health, but forward to something more complete—didn't come in a flash of lightning-like insight. It came quietly over an extended period of time, through moments of reflection and reassessment. Slowly, I began to fully understand the wisdom in the saying that *pain is inevitable, suffering is optional.*

All of us experience difficult situations in our lives. Some difficulties are financial challenges; some are relationship issues, illness, and worries about our physical being, or spiritual crises. Some of us struggle more in certain areas and less in others. But the root cause always involves us.

Whether it's something we thought, attracted, decided, or did, it always comes down to us. This does NOT mean it is our fault. We simply opened to it, were at the wrong place at the wrong time, had thoughts that somehow pulled something in, or—on a very subtle level—allowed it. When we realize this, and truly surrender to the truth of it, solution possibilities open. We move out of the thinking of blame and into the question of, "What can I do?" from a multidimensional perspective. Now possibilities for solution can include mental ones, like looking at the belief systems that may have created this, the emotions we might have suppressed that are finding their way to the top, the importance of giving our body what it needs, of our connection to the universe, and to how things affect our energy levels.

One of the reasons why it is so challenging to heal illness is that we tend to look at it in a unilateral way. We see the cause as physical and therefore the solution as well. That may be true if I break my arm, but what if I have a "mystery" illness such as fibromyalgia or chronic fatigue? Looking at issues from different vantage points and domains helps to not only break things down, but shows us where to act. When I speak of domains, I'm referring to the mental, emotional, spiritual, energetic, and physical aspects of our being. The mental reflects our inner thoughts and the conversations. The emotional amplifies the emotions we feel about something and how we handle those feelings. The spiritual is about our relationship with the Divine in all of this. The energetic is how all of this is held in the space around our body, given that our body doesn't actually end where our skin does. Our physical domain is how we manage all of this in our physiology and how imbalance manifests. Bottom line: <u>Even though symptoms and issues show up in the physical, they don't necessarily originate there. The problem and the solution are not always in the same place.</u>

The thing we often don't see in the difficulty of all of this is the possibility—the possibility for something else to come from the misery. This includes not only the learning we would prefer not to have, but the discoveries, the relationships, and the underbelly of gain that we encounter in even the most tragic of circumstances. The other day I asked a woman who'd lost her husband years ago if anything useful had come out of her experience. She said, "I never would have chosen it, but I'm so much more independent and full in my own life since he's been gone. I've developed internal and external skills I didn't know I needed. I'm a survivor in a way I wouldn't have been able to be otherwise."

Those who do know how to fail and rebound will make the subsequent learning work for them.

So, ultimately, how do we rise above these tumultuous waters in order to emerge as something or someone else? By going to the bottom first.

We're in the Way

I was with a girlfriend who'd put on twenty pounds while traveling for about two months. She kept saying that the weight would drop off after she got back home, but after she'd spent a month back in her world, nothing happened. So then she made it about the season. "It's summer," she observed. "You can't lose any weight in summer."

We choose not to see. We think that if we just lose ten pounds, everything will be easy. If lying doesn't work, or even if it does, we deny. Denial is another form of lying. We can blindly tell ourselves how what we did was okay or even how great we are in the midst of unacceptable behaviors, especially if it lines up with how we define ourselves. If we define ourselves as compassionate or kind and an opportunity to hide from that emerges, we might deny that the opportunity was there. **Once we see ourselves in a particular way, we reject the possibility of ourselves or other people seeing us differently from that viewpoint**.

Case in point: It was Christmas Day, 2010, a bitter-cold winter day. I was taking my dog to the local "impromptu" dog park up on the hill near my house. I met another friend there. Our dogs were playing when a third dog emerged. I whispered to my friend, "Be careful. Her dog is unpredictable." The dogs continued to play, and then, suddenly, a shriek bellowed from one of the dogs. We looked over to see the other dog on top of my friend's now-pinned-down dog, and it looked like he was going to have her dog for lunch. We ran over to separate the dogs. After inspection we saw that my friend's dog was bleeding. His right ear had almost been severed by the other dog's attack. The owner stood back, and from afar guiltily looked over. She peered at the injured dog, afraid to make a comment that might incriminate her undoubtedly responsible dog. After a few moments she made a paltry attempt to move things forward and seem helpful, "I have some antibacterial ointment at home if he needs it," she murmured.

My friend said, "He's going to need stitches."

She then turned more defensive and nervously exclaimed, "Well, we don't know who started it, so it may be your dog's fault."

My friend, trying to deal with the shock of her dog's injury, combined with the comment the woman just made, said, "If someone gets killed, does it matter who started it? Your dog attacked my dog and you're not taking responsibility. Dogs mirror their owners."

Well you'd think she would have cussed the woman out. Something about my friend making that comment was so out of line with the way the woman saw herself that she let loose. She screamed, "I'm still standing here, aren't I?! I'll have you know I take in rescue dogs and foster them! I have taken in over 250 dogs from around the area and I am a **good person**!"

My friend said, "Fine. I'll let you know via email what happens with my dog, and you can reimburse me for any vet charges."

They both left.

Afterward we found out that the woman's dog had bitten more than ten dogs in the neighborhood, and when we called the county to report the dog, we learned that she had been reported at least five times from other dog owners for similar behavior. But she couldn't take responsibility for what her dog had done or accept any assessments from others that were less than positive in nature, because that was in direct competition with the view that she was a "kind and compassionate person"(because she fostered rescues). The piece she couldn't see was that she was both. Yes, she was kind and compassionate to house the rescues, and she was also irresponsible when it came to dealing with issues involving herself and her dog's behavior. Oh, and do I even need to say this? She never reimbursed my friend for the vet bill. She ignored emails and any attempts to follow up on the injured dog's progress.

Because we often see ourselves one way, it is more challenging to recognize the multidimensional aspects of ourselves and what that might mean for our identity. So what if we're both? If we are really going to shift our ability to deal with situations as they are, we have to meet ourselves (including the negative parts) as we are. One simple and yet potentially challenging way to do this is to simply question, "Why did I do that?" or "Why didn't I?" and wait for the true response to emerge. If we are authentic with ourselves, the opportunity to see the other side of something emerges.

I had a client who said she wanted to be "successful" at self-employment. The reality was that she often slept in, didn't show up to meetings, and was late on projects. When I asked her why, she said, "Oh, I'm too busy and have too much on my plate." Every time I'd ask her that question, some "good reason" emerged. The problem was that these "good reasons" were blocking her from having what she said she wanted. Then I asked her to go a layer beyond by inquiring, "What's the fear, the real fear, behind you not acting in alignment with what you say you want?"

She thought for a moment and I could see her really reflecting; and with a pensive stare she looked up and said, "I'm afraid if I'm successful that people will look at me and be judgmental and critical. Sometimes it's better not to show up."

Interesting that she thought that not showing up would produce less criticism than acting. This is the bizarre pretzel logic in thinking that can cause people to act in incomprehensible ways. But once we have that understanding, we have something to work with. Now, with my client, we could work with the real issues instead of trying to devise surface strategies to shift what she didn't care about. We could push the fear to the side and not let it rule her. We could move it from being in front of her glasses (as the invisible thing she saw through) to something she could consciously put to the side and have in the background or not at all. From there we were able to unpack the elements that led to her fear, and through coaching she was able to completely change her pattern. She is currently very successful. This is the possibility that awareness leads us to.

Just having this basic awareness is useful in the simplest and the scariest moments of our day. You know that moment after you've had a car accident, or broken something badly, or heard some devastating news that you were not expecting? It's a breath where time stands still, logic is defied, and reality is redefined. That moment, once experienced, is often rejected and certainly resisted. Our inner dialogue is, "No, this can't be happening," or, "I won't accept this," or, "Make it go away," or, "Not now."

The problem arises when we take that momentary response and drag it out, letting it enter our daily experience. It becomes a theme for our life. We begin to organize our life around making something go away instead of stopping, seeing, and really paying attention to what's present inside ourselves, challenging our thoughts, beliefs, inner voices, and what we believe to be real. On top of that, we fight, dance around, or even ignore the basic ego needs that often interrupt our ability to see more clearly. These basic ego needs include: 1) the need for recognition or to be seen, 2) the need to be heard, 3) the need to be liked or included, and 4) the need for control.

Sometimes the difficulty is simply not seeing what we need. If we actually sat and asked ourselves, "What is it I need in this moment?" that simple question would eradicate unnecessary acting out and behaving around what we haven't acknowledged or articulated. For instance, if your relationship fails, it may be because you were not able to get your need to be heard met. Rather than seeing the real problem and perhaps being able to ask for what you want, the issue morphs into, "He didn't hear me," or, "I can't keep a relationship together." Or possibly, as it happened to one of my neighbors and to many others in the challenging economic climate as of late, she lost everything—her job, house, savings, and significant relationship. At the age of fifty she had to start over. She lost her sense of sanity, not only because of what happened, but because the basic need for control wasn't met, sensing that it was slipping through her fingers like water releasing through the faucet. Realizing one of these needs isn't being met can open us up and help to address the real internal issues that often aren't acknowledged or addressed. This realization doesn't make the outer concerns go away, it just illuminates the root of what's going on inside of us.

One of the largest challenges we face as humans is to see reality for what it is, to name what's happening, to feel what our experience of it is in our being, and to then act according to what supports us and those we love. As simple as it sounds, it's rarely what we do. The first step in seeing "what is" is to ask ourselves some questions that will move us in the right direction to unravel what is really happening. This will open the door to really tunneling through our difficulties and not only rising up, but ultimately going beyond.

Questions for Contemplation

1. Pick a situation you're dealing with. It may be small (trying to lose ten pounds) or larger (divorce,

bankruptcy, death, etc.). Are you in alignment or denial with it? If you're not sure, ask someone who knows the scenario. If it's denial, what will it take for you to be in alignment? Ask yourself, "What's the fear that may be keeping me from getting what I want in this scenario?" What are you afraid of facing?

2. What do you truly want to be rid of—a feeling, a thought, or a belief about yourself, someone else, or a situation? Identify it and make sure it's about *you* and not an outside person or circumstance.

Light at the End of the Tunnel

Keep this challenge you are experiencing present. Find the place in your being where you feel the pain. It may be your heart, your stomach, your lungs, or your throat. Give yourself permission to feel the pain associated with it for a few minutes. As you do this, feel what your heart is experiencing. Whisper the word "open" into your heart, making an *ahhh* sound on the first syllable. This will open the space deeper and allow the pain to begin to release. Now from this place, ask for help. If you are religious or spiritual you may pray, "Please God (or whatever name you'd like to use), help me release the pain held here in my being. I humbly ask for help and surrender to your guidance." Now simply sit. Let the Divine do its work. If you don't believe in a higher power, sit anyway and see what occurs. See if you can feel relief or an opening, or if guidance, wisdom, or direction emerges.

Chapter 2

What Were You Expecting?

Anger always comes from frustrated expectations.
—Elliott Larson

January 31, 2004
I've finally stopped fighting and am diving into the wounded discomfort, the pain, the weirdness. I'm spending hours meditating, seeing how deeply I can look into the cellular level of my being, hoping that as a metaphor I'll be able to see more into the core of existence.

Before, I wanted it to go away, but now I can invite its entry like a four-year-old would observe an ant in motion. It's so curious to have this way of experiencing the world that often I'm not sure whether to be grateful or angry. So I'm both.

Tonight someone called and said they saw my last boyfriend on the arm of a beautiful woman, totally in love. Having that information sent a knife through my heart. Then I questioned the pain. "Wasn't I over him?" "Why would I feel anything since so much time had passed?"

"I broke up with him, so how could I feel anything at this point?"

Then I realized I never fully felt the pain of the breakup with him. Every time I felt the pain, I did something to offset it, never fully allowing it to move through. I was living one of the two major reasons we have difficulty with emotional patterns. We're taught to do one of two things when we feel difficult emotions:

1. *Feel the difficulty of the emotion and ultimately transmute it so it goes on, transferring into healing for us.*

2. *Find ways to avoid the emotion, and in doing so keep the pattern embedded so that we are always acting in response to it, and on some level it is always controlling and manipulating us. "What you resist will not only persist, but present." There has to be a better way.*

What are expectations? According to the *American Heritage Dictionary,* to "expect" means to look forward to the probable occurrence or appearance of something, to consider likely or certain. Part of what makes a joke funny or a magic trick awe-inspiring is that we are expecting something other than what shows up. In those moments, the element of the unexpected surprise is a delight. But in life, not getting our expectations met is mostly disappointing and frustrating. If I think the moon is going to turn green tonight because someone told me so, then I will be sorely disappointed. If I structure my *day* around that expectation, it's not such a big deal; but if I structure my *life* around it, I've got a problem.

So, where do our expectations come from? They come from our parents, teachers, people we assess as knowledgeable in a certain arena, and the things we make up. I have many clients who expected that the job they took two years ago would look a certain way. Perhaps they might have the corner office, that all their work relationships would be great and everyone would be wonderfully nice, and they would be promoted within a two-year period. Sometimes they reach those expectations because someone, perhaps in a position of authority (the person who hired them) made that promise, or someone else mentioned it, or they even made it up themselves. But what if the person who hired them left within six months? Often any promise made by that person leaves with the person who made it. Now because that expectation wasn't met, the person walks with resentment, works with resentment, and lives with it as well.

I have met so many clients whose first words to me were about what was either directly or indirectly promised, or perhaps inferred, and never came to be. The person's expectations for the job molded around those expectations and, when they didn't manifest, a mood of resentment and often resignation took over. That mood begins to dominate and, if the person is in a position of power, possibly spread. Who wants to work in that office?

It happens in relationships as well. Betty got married in the mid '90s. It was her dream come true. She'd fantasized about this day for years. Her husband was an up-and-coming plumber who had dreams of making it big in the housing industry. They'd shared their dreams and together created expectations about how they would build their lives together.

While the larger dream about family and building something was well in place, what they neglected to speak about was what most people forget, and it's where a relationship often falls apart—the day-to-day stuff. What *he* neglected to tell her was that he expected to be able to go out with the boys after a long day of work, and kick back with them and a six-pack. What *she* neglected to tell him was that she expected him home for dinner every night to fulfill her view of what family life looked like.

She didn't say anything for a long time, but it came out in other ways. She started snapping at him for not taking out the trash and not clearing the table. He didn't want to hear it and so he stayed out later. She started spending more to get back at him, and he couldn't make enough to keep up. Eventually her resentment, and his, which was never directly spoken about, led them to a separation and bankruptcy. When they hit bottom they finally went to counseling, where these conversations were revealed, and for the first time in their relationship really got to spell out their expectations about marriage—what it should look like, feel like, and be like on a daily basis. They didn't get everything they wanted, but they were able to understand the other's pictures of what they thought it should be and negotiate those things that could ultimately lead to greater satisfaction in the relationship. As a result of that, they stayed together and recovered from their financial debacle.

So how do we know what our expectations are and how to ask for what we want? The place where you have pain, are triggered, or are angry, is typically a place where an expectation hasn't been met. A trigger is a feeling that my colleague Harvey Goldberg, an executive coach and international speaker on breakthroughs in performance, describes as, "Any event or stimulus in which our interpretation takes us out of a normal or happy state, and the reaction does not match the stimulus. An overreaction." When you are triggered there is no separation between you and your emotion. You essentially become the emotion you are feeling and therefore reaction is a short breath away. A common trigger for my clients is a boss who doesn't listen. Most of them never had a conversation with their boss from the get-go, or asked the boss what the expectations were, or told the boss what his/ her expectations of the job were.

One client in particular had lost motivation for a job he'd been in for about three years. When I asked him why, he said, "Things aren't good here." Now I had no idea what that meant, so I asked him to write down specifically what his expectations for the job included. It had to include a number, or something that was observable, measureable, or attainable. So, saying you want to work with "nice employees" is not something that can be observed or measured. Employees who say, "Good morning," five days a week is observable. It is something you can document and see. I had him write down a number of his expectations for the job. Here are a few he noted:

- Boss who would listen to me at least fifteen minutes a week
- Team members who met once a week to exchange information and concerns around projects
- A check-in every six months with an HR rep to see if I'm on track with my career goals
- A promotion every two years

Once you've named many, if not all, of your unmet expectations, now you can do at least one of three things:

1. Voice those expectations to the right person at the right time in the right mood.

2. Make requests around those concerns to elicit promises that will generate new actions that contribute to the expectations being fulfilled.

3. Take some kind of action that will move you in that direction.

With my client, we set up a meeting with his boss and did it in the context of a yearly review. He told the boss how he thought he was doing in the job and heard what the boss thought as well.

Then he said, "I'd like to go a level deeper and look at how we're operating on a day-to-day and week-to-week basis to see how we can be more efficient."

Boss said, "Great."

He went on to say, "What would help me do my job better is to have more contact with you. Right now, I'm lucky if I see you once a month. I know you've got a crazy schedule, and I'd like to sit down with you either on the phone or in person every week to spend fifteen minutes, getting your advice and feedback on what I'm working on. I believe that fifteen minutes could be a big payoff for the team by keeping us more on track and helping to meet the monthly goals more efficiently. Would you agree to that?"

The boss thought for a few moments, his eyes rolling around to see if he could make that commitment. At first he said, "If I do that for you, I have to do that for everyone."

My client asked, "Is anyone else asking you for this?"

The boss said, "No, they're not."

My client said, "Maybe they don't need it."

With that, the boss agreed to the weekly meeting. We went down the list and my client got everything he asked for except the agreement for the two-year promotion, but what he still got was that his boss knew he wanted to be thought of for the next promotion, so that when a position became available he was on the short list. With this conversation, many, but not all, of his expectations had been met; but more importantly, he cemented his relationship with his boss, got his deeper need for connection, and felt heard in the process.

Here's the lesson from this: before you enter into any agreement, contract, job offer, business arrangement, marriage, or any other interpersonal interaction: make sure you talk about the expectations, the spoken and the unspoken, the promises and the hopes, and be very clear about the commitments you are making. How many times have you gone to meet someone and you say, "I thought we were meeting about this," and the other person says, "I thought we were doing that..."

The Humane Society are organizations created for people who had unmet expectations and commitments that couldn't be fulfilled. The parents thought the kids would take care of the puppy, and the kids thought the parents would, regardless of what might have been said. Neither could keep his or her commitment; and they expected the dog would be easier to train, or take less time, or not chew on things. And sometimes you don't know. Sometimes it's a leap. When I got a dog as an adult for the first time, I had no idea what the commitment would be, but because the commitment was there, I adjusted. When people become parents they often have no idea what they're in for, but they do it because the commitment is there.

Ask yourself, "How can I be as clear as possible to know what I'm entering into? Who can I talk to who has had this experience? Will my commitment be there no matter what? Will my commitment change if my feeling about it changes?" To make sure that I don't feel disappointed or resentful when these expectations have not been met, what questions do I need to ask and of whom?

Some promises can't be made. Your spouse can't promise not to get sick, or that the economy won't tank. Life involves risk. On the other hand, we can mitigate much of what we find ourselves in by keeping the awareness of, and the conversation about, expectations alive, so that the trust, interaction, reliability, and sincerity in relationships remains alive and flourishing.

Having expectations is not a bad thing; we all have them. Knowing what they are, if they are realistic, and how they can be realized are what you want to keep in the forefront of your thoughts about expectations. Remember when you're upset about something, look to see what expectation you are holding that is being violated or simply not being met. Are you expecting that someone will listen to you, acknowledge you, or give you something? Is that expectation realistic? Can you let it go? Can you get it another way? These are all questions that will move you out of the anger, resentment, and upset that accompanies your frustration.

Light at the End of the Tunnel

1. Pick one expectation you see you've had. It could be small or large.

2. See what you expected or wanted from that.

3. Pick one action you can take to lighten the upset:

   • Let go of the expectation.

   • Change it.

   • Make a request of someone to get some/all of it met.

Chapter 3

Helicopter Perspective

Strategy #1: Assess Reality

*Reality is that which, when you stop
believing in it, doesn't go away.*
—Philip K. Dick

January 30, 2004
*It's 6:14 a.m. and once again I've been up all night
without sleep, no relief in sight. The body shakes and
the nose reeks of candle perfume. The irony is that the
more the body shakes, the stiller the inside becomes. I've
had to learn to get stiller and stiller even in the moments
of the most upheaval. Things I would have been more
reactive to now faze me less. It's kind of ironic, as the
rest of the world gets more agitated, quietude reigns
inside me, and that becomes stronger. All I have to
hang on to is the true center, and yet I also understand
craziness in a whole new way.*

*I hear the faint call of sleep. Getting used to the
feeling of agitation has not been easy, but it has given*

me enormous compassion for others' difficulty, for the difficulty of life. It has allowed me to step back and observe, a luxury always available, but one that few have taken advantage of. Also, I've become aware of the nature of tiredness—how to be tired, but not fall asleep; how to fall asleep when not tired; how to get tired when you're not, and how wonderful tired is.

So how do you assess reality? How do you really get in alignment when something you don't like is happening? What are some ways to move you into "this is it," when every part of your being is screaming "no"?

Often, it can be as simple as acknowledgment. I have a friend who's a gifted body worker. She's seen all kinds of physical, emotional, and mental pain in her clients. One day she had a woman come to her who'd tried all kinds of different modalities for healing and couldn't get rid of a terrible pain in the lower part of her belly. She'd been to doctors, had x-rays, MRIs, sonograms, and nothing showed up. What was even more bizarre about it was that every spring the pain would get bad, so bad that it would make her almost deathly ill. By the time she got to my friend, she was beside herself. My friend looked at her and said, "What you're missing is permission."

She explained that often when we have a stressful or traumatic situation, we disconnect from ourselves or from the place where we may be experiencing pain. This disconnection is often done for survival reasons initially, but unless we give ourselves permission to go back and reconnect with the part that got disassociated, it becomes hard to repair the concern. Giving yourself permission to look at and examine reality, even when you don't like it, is the first step to moving through a difficulty. My friend Molly gave her client full permission to feel the pain and where it was located. She held a safe space and encouraged her to let go and gently move into that place of pain. And when she did, the most amazing thing happened. She got to a memory that had previously not been accessible to her.

In the spring of 1980, her client JoAnn was pregnant. It was her third child and she was excited about finally having the family she longed for. Then in the middle of her pregnancy, an awful thing happened. Her darling three-year-old son, Ben, was kidnapped. He disappeared for what felt like forever, and she discovered weeks later that he'd been murdered. Crushed but determined, JoAnn decided that because she had other children at the time, she couldn't allow herself to feel the pain of his death, in order to continue living. She stuffed away the reality of what she was dealing with and went on. Only the reminder had been there, not only in the spring when the anniversary arrived, but on a deeper level all the time. Once she realized what the pain was telling her, she was able to go into it, to go through it, to do the necessary physical, mental, emotional, and spiritual work to get to the other side. She did and it was fruitful.

My friend says that by aligning with the reality of what happened, allowing her body to feel that, for the first time in over thirty years, she has an opportunity to have a different relationship with that pain and her body at the same time. She is doing much better and has finally been able to put that pain behind her.

Simply acknowledging what is happening can free you from the pain of denial and sometimes can be the ticket to moving through what seems impossible.

Here's a technique I use to get people (my clients and myself) in the reality of a situation. I had a car accident a few years ago and this technique really came in handy. I learned from Somatic Coaching and Peter Levine's work that when trauma hits, the first thing we want to do is pretend that it isn't happening. We want to get out, to move, to normalize. When animals are traumatized, they shake because they feel afraid. They don't pretend it isn't happening; they feel the shake and, when the danger has passed, they stop. When my dog hears thunder, she shakes; and when it's over, she stops. The memory may still be there, but the experience is gone.

We often stop ourselves from feeling, shaking, or admitting what's happening. So the last time I had a car accident, instead of getting out of the car immediately to exchange insurance info, I sat. I let the upset of the moment go through my body. I shook and allowed myself to shake because I knew that, in that scenario, it was normal. I let the shaking spiral through my body like a DNA helix, experiencing its existence. After a few minutes, when the shaking had expressed itself, I got out and did the paperwork. This saved me from suppressing the upset and possibly getting post-traumatic stress disorder (PTSD) from the experience later on.

When the body isn't allowed to fully express the experience when the upset happens, it will find other ways to do so. PTSD is one of those ways. So how can you align and assess the reality of what you're experiencing? Here is a technique I call, "The Moving Through," to get you connected to and through the reality of the moment:

The Moving Through

1. Say to yourself, "Wow. This just happened. I'm feeling…"

2. Notice if there is any shaking, twitching, or movement in your body. Sit with that and let the shaking express itself. Consciously give yourself permission to free up the feelings, expressions, and movement. See yourself as a hose that water is making its way through. Let all of that flow through you and go out by way of your feet. Give it whatever time it needs.

3. Ask yourself: "How do I feel right now? Is there anything else I need to feel supported in this moment?"

4. When you're ready, reassure yourself by saying, "It's okay now. I can move on."

You may not know what else you need or even what you're feeling, but the fact that you are asking and acknowledging yourself in that way at a difficult time will help your being feel supported.

Once you do that, once you say, "This is happening," it opens the door toward aligning with and ultimately accepting that what hit you could not have missed you, and ultimately accepting a reality you did not consciously choose.

Chapter 4

What Hit You Could Not Have Missed You

Strategy #2: Accept Reality

*In some way, suffering ceases to be suffering
at the moment it finds a meaning.*

—Viktor Frankl

February 15, 2004

*A couple of people have asked me if I'm angry.
Interestingly enough, other than an outburst or two at
my mother for not being aware, I haven't been. I've
been frustrated, concerned, sad, terrifically frightened,
depressed at moments, but not predominately angry.*

*I attribute this to the primary inner conversation I've
had, which is, "This is just what's happening now. This
will change," and remembering times in my life when I
thought what was occurring would last. Then, since I
know it won't last, I'm able to say to myself, "See this as a
gift. It is a new way to experience life, even though I may*

not have consciously chosen this. It is an opportunity to see life outside its normal realm and ultimately create new appreciation."

When I woke up this morning and realized I'd slept through the night without biochemical help, I was ecstatic. Very few times did I wake in the morning ecstatic from sleep. I am and will be able to appreciate things and people I had previously taken for granted. Being deprived can be the most gracious gift if you allow it to be so.

We want out—out of our suffering due to this problem, situation, relationship, illness. We think if we can just solve this one thing, if we can just overcome this, lose that, or get this; then it will all be all right.

And it is. For ten seconds.

And then it's not again, because something new needs to be solved or overcome. All the while we're denying our piece in it. Your piece is not that you "created it"; it's that it is your experience. You're here. You can't be anywhere else than where you are for whatever reason. Before you go into the why or the how, you have to not only assess the reality, but really stand in what's happening, even if you don't align, want, or even accept it. This is what's happening. Assume there are no real accidents. Whatever has happened, is happening, or will happen is destiny. The "if only" conversation we've all imagined is painful and out of alignment with reality.

When destiny hits, most of us just try to tread water. We figure if we can keep our head above water, we'll be okay. That may be a good short-term strategy, but what ends up happening is that most people get stuck there, trying to continue to cope. After a while, stagnation or depression sets in, as nothing moves forward or backward. The reason this hits is because our thinking is, "This wasn't supposed to happen." The resistance fuels our inability to cope. Nothing feels as if it's ever going to get any better, and this is an opportune moment for an addiction of any sort to wiggle its way in, even if you have little predisposition to addictive tendencies.

I have a friend who lost her husband. After a month or so with no clear healing or direction, she ended up getting involved with a convicted criminal, who, after dating her for a short while, kidnapped her, put a gun to her head, and forced her to agree to marry him. In order to move through the moment, she agreed and maneuvered through that compromising situation. Fortunately, she was later able to get out of the agreement intact. He ended up stabbing someone in the eye and landed back in jail for many years. His incarceration was a great relief to her!

These moments of extreme danger can present themselves when we have not fully realized, felt, and spoken the pain, disappointment, sorrow, anger, fear, and other emotions that linger inside our deep heart. In short, we often deny what is and, in the process, lie to ourselves.

The good news is that how you deal with destiny is what can be changed. We have the power of free will and free choice. We can begin to make a plan and take the first small steps toward moving into a new reality for ourselves, even if we don't know what that looks like yet. As simple as it sounds, most people live in resistance to their own pain, and it is the resistance that prevents them from experiencing real healing. As one of my teachers says, "The deeper the feeling, the deeper the healing." When you deeply surrender to the pain present in your heart, and from that place ask for the Divine's assistance, then the combination of surrender and acquiescence lifts what seems impenetrable and too heavy a burden. The assistance may also not come on your timeline. I remember being on the floor in the deepest prostration possible, asking, begging, and pleading for help with disabling migraine headaches in the late '90s, and the answer didn't fully reveal itself for a few years after that. I can't tell you exactly how or when, but it works.

For me the methodology that works best I amended from a teacher I studied with in Israel. It is what I call PATS. It stands for Praise (the Highest), Ask (for what you want), Thank (for what you have and will be given), and Surrender (to the Will of the Divine). First you want to (P) praise; if you're spiritual, bring in the Divine. All you are doing here is acknowledging a greater power. If you don't believe in a greater power, but believe in the force of nature or something else, bring that in. The idea is to see yourself in the context of something larger. You are recognizing your ant-likeness in the universe, which brings in a sense of humility.

Then, from this more humbled position, you (A) ask for what you want. You ask from your deep heart. You ask as if everything is at stake from this asking. You say, "Please help me to…" "I beg you to…" In the process, ask to dispel beliefs that have perhaps placed you or kept you in this scenario. To really uproot a pattern, the beliefs have to go as well. I've seen people reverse illness, find love, and release pain as a result of this kind of asking.

Then you (T) thank. Thank the Divine for listening, for granting, for all that has been given and all that will be. The gratitude will bring in more gifts, more blessings, and more love. Because we are not demanding, but asking for help, we have to be willing to be open to what shows, even if it is not in the form we might chose it to be in.

Now you (S) surrender to what happens. Now you let go and be open. Now you can act from a place of service to the highest.

One of the reasons this is powerful is that the obvious act of acknowledging and asking for help with what is bothering you is often what's in your way. Sometimes the biggest problem is the feeling about the problem. Last week I was in a coaching conversation with a client who's getting ready to move. We couldn't even get to the business issues we needed to discuss because she was obsessed with hearing back from a potential landlord on an apartment she wanted. So I asked her, "What are you upset about?" She introduced a whole line of scenarios: "What if someone else wants the apartment? What if they didn't like me? What if my employer didn't give a good recommendation?"

The mental level of tizzy was dizzying, and it had turned her into an emotional wreck. This is what we do; we mentally spin scenarios, get upset about those potential scenarios (which not only have not happened, but usually never do), spin more scenarios, and find ourselves in a state beyond repair. Now we need a rescue team to pull us out. For some it could be substances, food, or shopping, but the bottom line is that we can't "be" with what we've made up that feels real. This is where she was.

So I played the other side of her tizzy. I asked, "What if the landlord was so busy that she hasn't had time to get to your application and it has nothing to do with you? What if the recommendation was fine and you just don't know anything yet? What if no news is good news?"

She said, "Oh, I never thought of it like that." She calmed down, and the next day she got the news that the apartment was hers.

Sometimes, if you just align yourself with another potential reality, you can shift the emotion you've created and you don't even need to go any further. Sometimes creating emotion can be a habit and not necessarily something that serves you. Check to see whether the emotion you are feeling is something that is based in reality or a byproduct of something your mind may have made up. Knowing the distinction between emotions based in reality versus fantasy can change your emotional life.

Questions for Contemplation

1. What does seeing "that which hits you could

not have missed you" show you about your experience?

2. How does thinking this way serve you?

Light at the End of the Tunnel

For a moment, feel that everything in your life is happening just as it should; that there is no way anything could be different than what it is right now. Let yourself be fully in the moment of what it is, where you are, where your breath is, how you feel in your chair, bed, sofa, etc. Know that this is exactly how things must be in your life, whether you like them or not—that this is how they are. Be fully in the "are-ness." You may feel relaxed; you may feel resistance arise; you may want to cry; or you may just be, but the fullness of the "are-ness" will prepare your being for the next step, allowing you to access free will in being and acting. It's now time for change.

Chapter 5

Finally Feeling

Strategy #3: Fully Feeling Starts Fully Healing

If you are trapped in a nightmare, you will probably be more strongly motivated to awaken than someone who is just caught in the ups and downs of an ordinary dream.

—Eckhart Tolle

*F*ebruary 20, 2004

Will. Does it matter how much will you have, if all of it, or more of it, does any good? Tonight I'm out of whack again. Shaking from a day of too much, and my will is working against me. It wants me to stay up and work, but my body fights and calls me to bed. Will got me into this mess to begin with. I want to do it all, love pushing, want what I want. Will has also been a friend, but at what point does one differentiate between friend and foe? How do you know when to say no? As the rumbling calms a bit, I find myself once again surrendering to who's in charge, or what force directs me. Somehow I'm being shaped by this experience, as I know I'm not the same person I was when

I woke up this morning. Life has already shaped me today. What will appear tomorrow?

We are all shape-shifters, adapting and reacting to our physical, emotional, and spiritual experiences, positive and negative. When something joyful or something traumatic happens to us, it reshapes us on a cellular level. And when we are physically, emotionally, or spiritually ill, it's on the cellular level that we must begin to heal. That healing begins with the will to heal, with calling up all those reserves of will and determination that we never know we have until we need them. How often have you heard about people in the most dire of situations who, after they've come through, admit, "I never knew I had it in me"?

Resistance is something that happens naturally when we work out. It's a healthy part of the process. Not so when it comes to feelings. The more you resist, not only does it persist, but it actually grows; because now you have to navigate, act, react, and interact around the feeling that arises. It's harder in the short term and better in the long to just acknowledge it, feel it fully, understand where it's coming from, and donate it to a higher power. The trick is to meet it fully and let it go, not rehearse it to keep it alive. Oftentimes when something makes us angry, we feel the anger and then keep rehearsing the thing that made us angry, reinforcing and recycling the anger and never having it dissipate. In order to really meet something fully, we have to do the following "Feel it Out" strategy:

1. Realize you are feeling depressed, sad, angry, frustrated, crappy, or any other emotion that you would prefer not to be.

2. Say to yourself, "I'm feeling…" What this does is take you out of the role of "victim" of the feeling and puts you more in the observer seat, not to avoid it, but to be able to navigate its destiny. When you do this, think of yourself as watching a surgery from the observation room overhead. You are seeing the surgery take place, naming the aspects and parts of the operation, but you are not actually in the room. This allows you to meet, but not fall victim to, the feeling that is present. Here you can begin to be curious about it. A few questions I like to ask are:

   - Why does this bother me so much?

   - What does this remind me of?

   - What is this showing me I care about?

3. Now you can go deeper. Since you're now in more of a relationship with what's present for you, the moment for real healing is presenting itself. When you meet someone for the first time, you probably shake the person's hand before you feel comfortable enough to hug. Now you can hug. Put all other distractions to the side for a few minutes and give yourself the luxury of seeing how fully you can feel this emotion. Give yourself

permission to experience the feeling at the deepest level possible in your being. Notice all the places in your physicality where you feel this. Is it primarily in your heart, in your gut, or even in your lower back? Allow the feeling and its place to come alive. It can be scary to do this, but know that feeling this will not kill you. Know that this is where your possibility lies. Meeting the feeling and being in a relationship with its fullness gives it the freedom to express and to live through you. This expression is its opportunity for liberation. Give yourself the gift of this for a few minutes.

4. Now bring the Divine, the universe, God, Jesus, Allah, Hashem, or anyone/anything that you deem to be of a greater force than yourself. Ask for help. Say, "Dear— , I am sitting at your feet. You alone can help me. I need your help. From the bottom of my heart, I ask for your blessings, for your deliverance, for your power in helping me move through this painful and debilitating feeling. Please take this from me." Sit with that. Offer what you are feeling to the highest.

5. Lastly, to support the Divine in supporting you, feel into the place where you have been feeling the pain. Open that space by bringing the *ahhh* sound into it. The *ahhh* sound has been proven to open formerly closed spaces. The Aum (Om) sound, Allah, Adonai(in prayer), and other ancient

sacred sounds from different cultures contain the underlying syllables that make up this sound. Use the wisdom in this moment to support the process and open the place where the pain has been held, and release it. Sit with your prayer and this sound (you can start by saying it out loud and then bring it internally) until you find it shifting, dissipating, and a relaxed, calm feeling coming over you.

What you will notice as you do this is that, as you feel and release it, the feeling will lose its grip on you. You may not get it all on the first try, but you should notice a feeling of calmness overtake you. Sometimes the feeling will go away completely on the first try, and sometimes it's held in layers. Be patient with yourself and allow it to move through you as it's ready. Honor what's coming up inside and give it permission to let go. You will be amazed at how powerful this simple exercise can be. Practicing this can transform your emotional life. Being in a relationship with what is present for you, speaking it when necessary, feeling it for the sake of moving it through, and ultimately dancing with emotions as a way of life, will have an impact on every part of your inner and outer life. It will change the way you relate to others, enhance the honesty with which you speak, and as a result the destiny of those relationships. But even more than that, getting honest in that emotional way really sets the stage for the most important conversations you will ever have— the conversations you have with yourself.

Questions for Contemplation

1. What feelings have I been avoiding?

2. Other than the obvious reason of "it's uncomfortable," why have I done that? What reward has it gotten me?

3. What has been the cost to myself of not feeling?

Light at the End of the Tunnel

Pick something that you may have been avoiding thinking about or feeling. Apply the "Feel it Out" strategy outlined above. Give yourself space to notice reactions in your body and how you feel about yourself afterward. Notice in the days that follow what other things either open up, or perhaps call you to feel. Often, after we peel away one layer, another one emerges. Know that it is part of the process, and address it as you are ready; but address it.

Chapter 6

The Thinking That Got You In Won't Get You Out

Strategy #4: Redirect Your Thinking

The world breaks everyone and afterward many are strong at the broken places.

—Ernest Hemingway

February 27, 2004
At my mother's insistence I went to see a traditional allergist to determine what I'm allergic to and can be treated for. After describing my symptoms in detail for close to an hour, the resident looked at me and said, "I've never heard of this. I think we need to put you on an antidepressant."

"But I'm not depressed," I rebutted, "or if I am at all, it's because of this physical condition."

His response? "Antidepressants are used for many things." And once again I realized that I'd encountered someone who decided my syndrome didn't exist because he didn't intimately know it. He assumed my symptoms were psychosomatic in nature and ultimately without merit. Back to the acupuncturist.

After two treatments this week, a small victory—I've slept the last two nights without interruption and without the aid of any sleep inducer, natural or otherwise. After three months of predominately sleepless nights, this is a place where I can measure progress.

Now being somewhat more coherent, I'm noticing what I haven't been able to notice before. In fact, what most of us never pay attention to: the shape of the branches of the trees outside the house; the fly crawling on the window, wondering if it has a distinct personality, and if so what it's like; the way the shadow from the trees hit the road and how it changes at differing times of the day.

I never realized how much the outside world parallels 42nd Street in New York City. It's just that I have to notice the movement in order to really see it; it won't impose itself on me.

The other day I was driving by a FedEx truck on a windy day. From around the back of the truck emerged its driver with a stack of boxes. He got about twenty feet from the truck and they all succumbed to the force of the wind. I watched his face to see who this man was. He started laughing and laughing, and his body surrendered to the reality of the moment. I drove up to him, rolled down the window, and yelled, "Great attitude!" He laughed even more. While this reaction may not be appropriate for many incidents, this behavior came out of the conversation he had with himself in the moment it occurred.

The questions you ask and the conversations you have with yourself determine the destiny of your moment and ultimately your future. They put you on the path of either impossibility or probability. The questions you ask when things happen are a bigger reflection of you than what you experience, because they define who you are under stress. When you work out and the muscle is stressed, that's when the muscle gets defined, but it's strained in the process. As an old friend used to say, "It's not what happens to you, but what you do about it."

Questions to Ask

1. How can I use this?

2. What is this teaching me?

3. How does this serve my soul?

4. What does the Divine want me to know?

If we operate from the premise that everything is good, even when it doesn't feel that way, then the questions that arise from that premise are supportive and move us in a direction that serves instead of punishes, and this better affects our ability to deal.

I had a coaching client, Roland, who was in a very depressed state. In the mid-2000s, when the housing market was booming and out of control, he divorced his wife, sold his half of the house, and claimed his freedom. He was worried about his financial future, so with the money he had he made down payments on a few condos and a house. He mortgaged himself heavily, and then he lost his job. By 2007, the market had changed. Prices he was sure would climb fell like timber. Finding a job became close to impossible. He was teetering. He began to spend days inside what would soon be the bank's condos. He began to drink. Within a matter of months he lost everything. At fifty he needed to start over, but he couldn't. When he finally got to me, we initially talked about the kinds of conversations he was having with himself. He told me his predominant question was, "Why me?" and his answer was, "Because you're an idiot and you deserve it for the stupid decisions you've made."

When people feel they "deserve" what's happened, it creates a deep hole from which it is difficult to dig out. He was angry for having made the decisions that he did, but deservedness locked in the anger even deeper. Swimming in a sea of thoughts, leading to unsupportive emotions that were unacknowledged, the actions he took fueled his spiral. He found himself lying on the bottom, drowning in his own ocean of thoughts, emotions, and bad decisions, unable to feed off of anything but his own sorrow.

As we continued our sessions, we acknowledged his emotions. Most people act from, dance around, and deny what they are feeling. This acts like boiling water with a lid on, a constant bubble, hot under the surface; and it cooks or burns anything that enters it.

The opportunity to really feel it ushers it through, and the power it holds begins to disseminate. With the help of a few supplemental techniques such as Sufi healing and EFT, the emotions were able to move to the side and not rule his opinions of himself. We then were able to really examine and rework the inner conversations he was having with himself. Out of the new conversations, a new reality began to appear. He felt new possibilities emerging. At about this time, he was in Starbucks for his usual morning coffee. As he sat reading the paper, an attractive forty-something woman sat down and they began chatting. They talked politics, spirituality, kids, and life. Two hours flew by. As they parted she asked, "What are you doing for dinner tonight?"

They were married about nine months later. She is a successful doctor, and while he is not perfectly financially stable yet, he now has a partner who can support him and who he enjoys supporting in many ways as well. When I talk to him now, he is happy. There is richness to his life that was not present before, and that richness has been the foundation from which he's been able to rebuild his future. (If you're interested in knowing more about coaching and how it can serve you, go to my website: www.sandracrowe.com to find out more.)

Every complaint is an underlying request.

One of the simplest and most life-altering lessons I learned while training to be a Sufi healer was to feel my emotions. As basic as that might sound, most people don't do it. They react, deny, overlook, cover up, and dance around them, but mostly don't really feel them. Yet this is the key to really moving through them. Nobody wants to feel bad, physically or emotionally. Yet denying those feelings is like moving fat around. For a moment it looks good, but it's still there. The more we listen to ourselves, the easier it is to have more awareness of our inner emotional life. Two questions I learned to ask in this process are:

1. What am I feeling?

2. What need isn't being met?

Feelings and needs go hand in hand. When our needs don't get met, we get upset, calculating, quiet, covert, angry, etc. When we dive in, we are able to either give ourselves what we need or ask for what we want. One of the most common places this shows up is with complaints. People tend to complain about things when what they really want is either for someone to listen to their concerns or to make a request for something that could help them.

When you're upset there's something that you want that you're not getting. How can you put that into words? In relationships, I've found that some of the easiest ways to ask are: "Would you be so kind as to—?" or, " I would love if you would—" "Would you do that for me?" or even, "What would it take for us to make that happen?" When you make a request it can move you out of a complaint dynamic into a valuable future. When you do this, make sure it has the following items:

- the person to whom you are making the request
- the thing you are requesting (make sure it's obvious)
- when you are requesting it by (ASAP is not a time)
- conditions for satisfaction—be specific (how will they know they are giving you what you want, how you want it?)

If these items aren't present, you may not get what you want and you're liable to blame the other person. If you can't get what you want from someone, ask someone else, or ask at another time. The key to getting what you want is to ask the right person, at the right time, in the right place, and in the right mood. When I wrote my first book, *Since Strangling isn't an Option...* I wanted to interview some well-known people to find out how they dealt with difficult people. I ran into Betty Buckley, William Hurt, Lulu, and Harvey McKay, who wrote, *How to Swim with the Sharks Without Being Eaten Alive*. I made the request of each of them, and they did not want to participate; but I got something out of the interactions with each of them. Because I kept requesting, I was, in fact, able to interview Felicia Rashad and Michael Deaver, and obtain great testimonials from Ken Blanchard and Brian Tracy. Don't be shy about making requests. Feel good about taking the risk. Most of the time, there's little to lose and most people will respect you for it.

This is a very critical skill when it comes to being able to move through difficult situations and moments. Most of the time, we cannot move through those situations alone. If you follow the six degrees of separation rule, you probably know someone who knows someone who can help you make something happen. Many times you can avoid the uncomfortable social situation of putting someone on the spot by making the request via email. It gives them time to think about it without feeling pressure to respond immediately. If they say no or if they don't know, let them off the hook by asking for someone else they might recommend.

One of the largest contracts I've had to date as a speaker/trainer came as a result of a client who wasn't able to hire me; and when I asked for other referrals, she recommended an organization I've now been doing business with for five years. Making a request can open doors you didn't even know were there.

Bottom Line Questions to ask Yourself

1. What am I feeling?

2. What do I need?

3. What requests can I make?

Questions for Contemplation

1. How does thinking about what I feel, need, and want help me to feel more satisfied?

2. What are the concerns I have in making requests?

3. How can I do it anyway?

Light at the End of the Tunnel

Take a moment to assess your body. How are the grounding mechanisms that hold you centered doing? In other words, are your feet stable and solid on the ground? Can you feel your center (two fingers below your belly button)? Just thinking about these places, these spots of stabilization, will bring you to a place where you can be more centered and increase your awareness.

Take a deep breath in and release. Now notice anything you are complaining about or are unhappy about. Is it something you can change? If not, what do you need to do to let go or distract yourself from thinking about something that is of no benefit? If so, what steps do you need to put in place for something else to arise out of that? Who can help you? What requests can you make to help you move this issue forward? Notice any fear or trepidation around making the requests, but don't let it stop you. Feel good about the fact that you are making the request, and don't over-focus on the outcome. Trust that you will get what you need. Know that this will happen one way or another.

Chapter 7

Difficult Interactions with Self

Strategy #5: Interact with YOU Differently
The off-center, in-between state is an ideal situation,
a situation in which we don't get caught, and in which
we can open our hearts and minds beyond limit.

—Pema Chodron

July 25, 2004
Life in the chemical sensitivity lane has gotten a bit easier. As long as I go nowhere, see no one (with any chemical products), breathe as little as possible, and minimally exert myself, things are fine.

Today my big scare was the next-door neighbors painting the outside of their home. Yes, even the paint from an exterior source can be detected by my talented olfactory system. When my housemate told our next-door neighbor I had a few sensitivities, she replied, "Oh, yes, my son has allergies, too." But when she told her that these were not ordinary allergies, that she had to sit on top of me to keep me from convulsing because my nervous system was so overly stimulated, the neighbor's eyes began to widen. When she told her I had to sleep outside in my car because my friend had put on too much hair product that day, she began to get it. "This is no ordinary allergy" was an understatement, she was beginning to comprehend.

Today I also had a haircut. Maggie was kind enough to come to me on her day off. As she cut my hair, she asked, "Aren't you going crazy from having not gone out or done anything?"

"Sometimes!" I replied. "And sometimes it's actually a bit of a relief."

In a certain way I think we all would like a self-imposed vacation from our life at times. Mine happens to be a bit more extreme and extensive than most people would choose, but it is giving me the opportunity to appreciate the simple in a way that's not only hard, but really impossible to achieve when we are on autopilot.

A tree looks more climbable, a river dunkable, a rock more throwable, all because I'm able to stop and appreciate their energy in a way I couldn't or wouldn't have before. Nothing makes me happier than slow walks, relaxing drives, and meeting with nature that wouldn't be available in the same way. Cherishing the subtle has become a way of life. For this I am grateful.

It's important to realize that language is an action. Most of us think of speaking as passive, a way of using sound to express thought or to communicate a need.

But language is more than an agent of our brain. It sets mood, creates emotions, and forges bonds or enemies with others. When we speak, we set a whole series of reactions in motion.

In order to interact with yourself differently, you have to identify the kinds of conversations you have with yourself and make them more deliberate. What happens when you think? Take ten seconds of blankness. What emerges? Are you able to observe yourself thinking? The conversations outlined here will help you define the kind of thinking and the thoughts that will help you have more productive inner conversations.

Inner conversations. Where do they come from? The obvious answer would be that they originate inside us, but think about that for a moment. We don't come into this world with these conversations already in place, do we?

Most of our inner conversations have their origins in what others have told us about ourselves. These may be things our parents have said, or the other kids in school, or our first boss, or the marriage partner who suddenly stopped loving us. So, a big piece of inner conversations needs to begin divorcing ourselves from old, negative conversations that may not belong to us.

Everyone who has ever hurt us has contributed to our inner conversations, and everyone who has ever loved us has, too. Part of learning how to talk to yourself effectively is learning how to filter the residue of conversations with others so that what you're left with is balanced, nurturing, and positive.

This means rejecting the extremes. If you were always told as a child that you were worthless, recognize that the voice that speaks is not yours. Our inner conversations have history and consequence in our outer actions. Other people's conversations with us often become our own. Someone telling us, "You're bad," becomes, "I'm bad." When you're in a tough place, the conversations you have with yourself can be your strongest and most valuable resource or your biggest enemy. The conversations you have and the mood you have them in will either take you where you want to be or leave you where you are. Here's what they look like.

Conversations of Observation and Assessments

From the time we're children, we begin to make assessments about ourselves and the world we live in. By assessments I mean opinions, judgments, or decisions about how things are. Some of those assessments, such as prejudices against others or pride in our ethnic background, are given to us by the adults in our world. For instance, "The US is the best country to live in" is adapted mostly by people who live in the US. Others we get from our own experiences and intuitive judgments ("I'm good at dancing," or, "I'm terrible at dancing."). Eventually, we become very adept at making these assessments or judgments as if they were observations. What's the difference? We might say, "Spring is the best time of year," rather than acknowledging that really, "Spring is MY favorite time of year." It's my preference, but I may see it as THE TRUTH instead of my preference. In reality, spring is just another season, and as soon as you make it better than something else, you've put a spin on it.

When we report something we've seen on the news, that's an observation. When we say how terrible or wonderful that thing is, we've moved from the realm of reporting it to the realm of assessing it. "I have a red car" is an observation, a fact. "I have a jazzy-looking red car" is an assessment—that is, a judgment, an expression of what I believe to be true. I might go a step further and say, "Since I have a jazzy-looking car, then I am better than everyone else," which is another assessment. As soon as we give it flavor—like, dislike, good, bad, better, worse—we have taken it out of the realm of observation and moved into the world of assessments or opinions. In that world, we invite difference of opinion, agreements and disagreements, and, potentially, allies and foes. There's nothing wrong with making assessments; simply acknowledge that you are doing so and that your assessment is indeed yours, and while it may feel like THE truth, it is, in fact, YOUR truth.

Observations can often be pushed aside by assessments. My friend Carl is fifty-two years old and has never been married. He's convinced there's something fundamentally wrong with him. Our beliefs come from our assessments. His assessment? "I'm fundamentally flawed because I'm not married." His belief? "I'll never be able to get married now." This belief isn't the truth; it's an assessment he made based on a value system created at a young age by Carl's parents and peer group. As long as he continues to hold this belief, he will continue to produce the same result, which is not being married.

Therefore, assessments reinforce reality. The opposite can be true as well. "I have three red cars," which is an observation that may cause me to assess that "I am rich," because my definition of rich is having three cars. Being able to separate and define what your beliefs are, and where they come from, will help you to unravel the core assessments and beliefs from which you operate and judge yourself and others.

When we speak to ourselves, we not only describe the way we observe our reality, but we generate new realities and make things happen accordingly. So if my friend Carl says to himself, "My history is not having been married, but my future can hold marriage," his possibility for generating new realities has now shifted. The supportive questions to ask him (your) self are, "What do I believe that is causing me pain or may be blocking my future?" "What do I need to do to change that, and shift my actions or my beliefs?" If you take new action, and get a new result, that may shift your belief, or you can shift your belief in order to take new actions. I find that trying on new beliefs, like trying on new clothes, helps to open the door to new actions and, ultimately, new results.

If my friend Carl thinks, "I'm going to try on the belief that I could get married and have the life of my dreams, whatever age I am, and really live from this right now," that could open the door to new actions and results being available for him that were not before. The more we are aware of the conversations we live and act from, the more possibility we have to direct and redirect them.

Conversations Generated by Breaking Points in our Lives

These are moments that interrupt our existence in powerful ways. For example, the news of being diagnosed with cancer. These are the standout moments, the ones with memory. How we deal with breaking points is how we deal with life. Life is not just about getting rid of breaking points; it is also about learning to deal with them. When things don't go smoothly, the normal reaction is to curse the moment, and this can trigger our reactions to our situations. The supportive conversation to have here is, "Stop. Breathe. I can deal with this." Sometimes these moments will initiate shaking or a feeling of, "It's too much."

Borrowing from Peter Levine's book, *Waking the Tiger*, shaking, or trembling, is a normal response to intense moments as our autonomic nervous system kicks in—just as with animals when they are confronted with fearful moments. His advice? When we have bad news, accidents, or other traumatic moments, let the shake happen. This facilitates the flow of fear through the body and allows you to recuperate faster. Notice the conversations flowing through you in these moments, but don't do anything with them unless you need to act to get out of a dangerous situation.

There is an entire realm of treatment called Somatic Therapy based on this concept of being in your body, feeling the sensations, and letting the natural flow of fear move through you. In many cases, PTSD arises because people chose to keep moving during/right after a traumatic event, and the incident literally got stuck in their nervous system and kept replaying the scene again and again. If you can allow the sensations to move fully through you at the time of trauma, you can avoid that reaction.

Conversations of Entitlement

These could also be called conversations of resentment. We all believe that we're fundamentally equal to the next person and that it's our natural right to pursue happiness. Even though we live with that cultural conversation, in reality we live in a society where there's economic imbalance. If you're not careful, this conversation can also lead to a sub-conversation of resignation, where no possibility is generated or conceived. Often we feel we deserve more than we are getting, especially as we compare ourselves to others. "That's not fair" offers the opportunity for a more supportive conversation of, "That's what IS right now. Now what?" or, "What can I do so I feel my needs are being met and I'm not concerned with others?" or if you're spiritual, "What can I pray about and ask the Divine for assistance in and then take action on?" That conversation will move us out of entitlement and into serving ourselves and our higher needs. Conversations of entitlement tend to be more about comparing ourselves to others and looking to see how their things compare to ours. Focusing on what's possible will take you out of the conversation of entitlement or resignation and move you into possibility.

Conversations for Possibility

If you take the road of, "Now what?," then possibility becomes inevitability. Now you need to have the right conversations with the right person at the right time in the right mood. In order to have them with others, you have to recognize the need within yourself. "I need to brainstorm this with someone. I'm coming up short, when it's just me." So when you have them with yourself—or even others—declare it. Say, "I'd like to have a brainstorming conversation (with myself)" and put it on your calendar: today at 2:00 p.m. I am meeting with myself for fifteen minutes to think about, mind map, outline, or ponder. It will give structure and creativity to how you want to solve problems and difficulty in your life. If you come up short with yourself, think, who can I direct this conversation with externally? Now you can identify the missing pieces and those who can help you with them.

Conversations for Action

Once we've realized we need to do something, how and with whom do we coordinate action? The questions here are, "With whom?" and, "By when?" Without those pieces in place it will be hard to move forward. Sometimes it's helpful to ask someone else to hold you accountable and you can do the same for them. A supportive book on this topic is, *Who Will Do What by When? How to Improve Performance, Accountability and Trust with Integrity* by Tom Hanson, PhD, and Birgit Zacher Hanson, MS, which can help you take these distinctions further.

Three Basic Moods about Life

A good friend of mine has a little boy who's almost eight years old. Jeff is a good kid, sweet, bright, and well-adjusted. But if you asked me to think of the word to describe him, that word would be morose, or melancholy.

Jeff was born with a host of physical problems that made the first year of his life a hellish round of operations and procedures. He had trouble breathing and sleeping, and sometimes he couldn't swallow food. He cried all the time because he was thoroughly miserable.

Today, Jeff has no physical problems, other than an occasional soccer bruise. But he also doesn't have that light, happy, giddy, childlike quality that most eight-year-olds have.

Jeff's assessment of life, forged in his first year, is that life is hard and painful. At the age of eight, his inner conversations are very basic, but they're still framing his assessments and feeding his lower-energy mood. As he gets older, he'll have an opportunity to shift that, if he can see where he is, and discover that his inner conversations mold his mood. He may be able to declare new conversations and attitudes from which he'd like to live.

Each of us lives our life in one of three basic moods, and by moods I mean the underlying attitude from which we see the world. These moods are created from the fundamental assessments we make about our lives, beginning in our childhood. While these moods may flavor the way we see things, we are not bound by their historical impact. Once you realize a general mood you live from, you can begin to change your inner conversation around it.

Possibility mood: positive, optimistic, energetic, ambitious about the future

Even-keeled mood: solid, grounded, basic, present

Lower-energy mood: sad, negative, resentful, resigned about life, depressed, thinking about the past, or worried about the future

The language we speak influences our moods. For instance, the following is a list of irrational things we often say to ourselves when we're in a difficult situation or perhaps with a difficult person. These inner conversations either reinforce our mood or, if we recognize we're doing it, can completely shift it.

Irrational Repetitive Things we Say to Ourselves and How to Dispute Them

Repetitive: I can't stand this.

Alternative: What can I do to shift this?

Repetitive: This is the worst thing that could have happened.

Alternative: Okay, this is awful. How can I fully be with it? Now what?

Repetitive: I'm such an idiot for letting this happen.

Alternative: I get to make mistakes like everyone else. What can I learn so as not to repeat it?

Repetitive: I'll never learn how to do this.

Alternative: I've learned how to do other things, so I know I can learn how to do this. With what do I need help?

Repetitive: Why does this stuff always happen to me?

Alternative: I keep making the same mistakes, so the results are the same. How can I get out of this pattern?

Repetitive: He never returns my calls. She's always too busy to talk when I call.

Alternative: Who knows what's going on with him/ her; I'll stop waiting for what may never happen and get on with my life. Who else can I call?

Repetitive: My neighbors are completely inconsiderate.

Alternative: Instead of grumbling to myself, I need to talk to them about what's bothering me and make a specific request.

Repetitive: Nobody cares about this issue but me.

Alternative: Other people care about this issue. I just need to seek them out. How can I do that? Maybe some of my Facebook friends might be interested.

Repetitive: Life seems so unfair to me.

Alternative: Good things have happened and they will again. What kind of conversation can I have to change the actions I'm taking and therefore my destiny?

Repetitive: I'm a terrible parent.

Alternative: I could have handled this situation better. The next time it happens, I'll be better prepared. How can I repair this and what can I do differently next time?

Repetitive: If I let someone else do this, it won't get done right. I must do it myself.

Alternative: I made mistakes when I started, and others helped me learn from them. I need to do the same for the people I'm supervising. What questions can I ask them to check their understanding? What do they need to get it done?

Repetitive: My boss is the world's worst.

Alternative: What requests can I make of him or her to make things better?

or

Alternative: Being this unhappy isn't healthy for me or the people I work with. I need to look for another job.

Future Think

My anorexia started in college when I was nineteen, after I put on "the freshman ten." Gaining that weight was a shocker. I felt as if I'd lost control over my body.

I wondered, "What else could I lose control over?" It terrified me.

When I looked in the mirror I heard one very powerful word: "Fat." My conscious self was sending the message that those ten extra pounds made me look awful. My unconscious self was sending the message that I was no longer in command of my body, which translated to not being in command of my own life.

So I took control. Some kind of switch got flipped in my brain and I went 180 degrees the other way. The force of will I'd put into eating I turned toward not eating. In effect, I began starving myself.

The intricacies of self-starvation are fascinating and frightening. I was the enthusiastic cheerleader of my own malnourishment. I was denying my body the nutrition it needed to function, and encouraging myself that I was doing the healthy thing.

At one point, I could manipulate my body in such a way that my stomach touched my back, I was so thin. (I went from 110 pounds to seventy-five.) And yet I'd look in the mirror and hear, "Fat." My internal conversation became masochistic. To demonstrate how disciplined I was, I'd dare myself to walk past a bakery and then say to myself, "I'm so above that." I also was bulimic, and would purge after eating. I saw desire, even the desire of my body for nourishment, as something negative, a weakness to be conquered.

When other people tried to talk to me about their concerns that I was dangerously thin, my unconscious self-translated their concern into bullying. Language defines our reality, remember? I was hearing, "We want to control you," not, "We care about you," and that became the truth for me.

What saved my life? Going to Paris for a summer abroad. One of the women on my trip had herself been anorexic and recognized the pattern in my behavior. Angela didn't stand on ceremony. She told me she knew what I was doing and why I was doing it. And she warned me how it could end. She described in great detail how she'd been put in the hospital and fed intravenously—in effect, force-fed, twenty-four hours a day. Describing how her arms were pinned down, her body forced to eat, and her life no longer her own, gave me a glimpse of what could possibly be in store for me. She told me how she had lost all her freedoms, including the most basic of them, deciding when and what to eat.

This was total loss of control—what I most feared. My mother had been threatening to put me into a facility, but I'd convinced myself it wouldn't happen. Coming face to face with someone who'd taken the same dreadful path I was stumbling down and hearing where it could go was a needed dose of reality. Angela's blunt, straightforward assertion—that I had two choices: stop myself or be stopped by others—threw cold water on my pattern and forced me to get more aligned with my reality and stop the "bleeding."

Of course there was a bump or two in my journey back to balance. My first reaction was to eat a lot of chocolate, which is a natural reaction, right? But I soon realized that binging on chocolate and then purging was a sickness, and one I didn't know how to deal with. I was far away from home, and really only had my own resources on which to fall back. So, I began to deal with it through conversations with myself. And in doing so I developed a process I called "Future Think."

Future Think is a way of holding the present and the future in the same parentheses with the question, "How will I feel if I do or don't do this?" I began to place myself in the future while still being in the present. As I sat in front of a half-gallon box of ice cream, for instance, I'd negotiate with myself. "Okay, you want to eat this whole half-gallon. But how will you feel after you've eaten it?" Immediately, feelings of remorse, misery, and disappointment arose. It was both the answer and the feeling. "So, how about eating just three tablespoons?" I negotiated. I found that eating just a little, if I ate it slowly and with awareness, satisfied me more than if I'd had too much or nothing at all. Part of being an adult human being is learning how to satisfy yourself by regulating your desires.

So I beat my anorexia one conversation at a time. Future Think was able to offset my entire pattern of eating. It wasn't immediate and it wasn't easy, but little by little it became a stronger and stronger tool, until finally my conversations with myself were the strongest resource I had in reestablishing my mental, emotional, and physical balance.

The Real Interior Design

As a longtime student of healing modalities, I'm interested in what works. As I studied different techniques, I found really valuable pieces in almost everything I did, but did not find that modality to be the "be all end all." So I took the pieces that worked and combined them. From Bruce Lipton and Candice Pert's research we know that emotions and reactions are not just in the brain, but in the entire physiology down to its cellular expression. We know that memories, while held in our past, still operate much of our behavior in the present. Thanks to Alex Lloyd and Gary Craig, we also know that by tapping certain points in the body, we can rewire old patterns of thinking and feeling. From the work of Lester Levinson, Sufi healing, and many meditation masters, it became evident that simply feeling emotions fully in the heart and inviting them through our bodies, honors what we had held for so long, and in a sense gives those old feelings the chance to move on when they no longer serve as a form of protection or reminder. And from the work of Karl Dawson, who invented Matrix Reimprinting we know that it's possible to review and rewrite our history in the field of our being, and as a result create new ways of reacting to old patterns.

From the questions, Why wait for feelings to happen?, What if you could actually design your feelings?, What if you could input ways of operating that ultimately serves you?, I created a technique called "FFORR Yourself," one that pulls the research, efficacy, knowledge, and usefulness of these modalities into one.

FFORR stands for: **Find it, Feel it, Open it, Release it, Rewire it**, and it works like this: Find an emotion that you are feeling that bothers you about a particular situation or person. It might be frustration, anger, sadness, or even depression. Become very aware of the emotion. Awareness is one of the most challenging things to do. Simply realizing that you are in some kind of upset, seeing yourself in it, instead of being in reaction to it, takes you a step away and opens the door to fixing the thing that got you there in the first place. Step one is to simply **FIND/ BECOME AWARE OF** the emotion that bothers you.

Step two is to actually **FEEL** it. As you feel it, you can get to know it a bit. Interview your emotion. Ask it, "Why does this bother me so much? Is it reminding me of something else?" When you do that, the emphasis is taken off of the upset and put back on you.

Step three is to **OPEN** up the emotion. You can do this by putting your hand on your heart, breathing through that space, and saying *ahhh* through your throat. The Institute of HeartMath research shows that by putting your hand over your heart, your compassion increases, and breathing through the heart helps to open it. We know that by saying the *ahhh* sound, the throat, which connects to the heart, opens, and it becomes easier to release trapped emotions which can be let out through the front or back of the heart. As you do this, it automatically takes you into step four: **RELEASE**. Here you just want to stay with it, to let it move through and allow old emotions to make their way out. By simply recognizing and meeting the emotions, they give us a sense of permission to let go and free ourselves from their grip.

Now you can go to step five: **REWIRE**. Here you give yourself a new emotion to replace the old. Say you were feeling anger and you'd like to feel peace. With your hand still over your heart, you now imagine peace flowing through your being while your other hand touches the point on your hand in between your pinky and ring finger (on either the left or right hand). When the energy goes all the way through you, you simply sit, knowing that you have rewired something inside you. Now you can say thank you to yourself and the universe. The gratitude helps to imprint the new emotion. This technique I find to be helpful whenever you are in a state that doesn't serve you, that takes you places you would prefer not to be, and you need to reorient yourself very quickly. You can do it almost anywhere, with ease and efficiency. Try it right now.

When you become an observer of your inner conversations, everything starts to make sense. You see the connectedness between your inner ability to think, conceive, and create, and your outer ability to generate results. Once that link is made and your inner life becomes more vibrant and deliberate, from there you can begin to regulate, design, and yes sometimes even control not only the inner, but the outer conversations as well.

Now that we know more of what drives our actions, we can begin to shift how the inner thoughts and conversations drive our outer conversations as well. Since every outer conversation has some kind of purpose behind it, even if it's just to chat to reinforce that relationship, we can begin to drive our outer conversations more succinctly, with more pinpointed purpose and more awareness of our final destination in the interaction.

We can now begin to shift our focus to the more outer conversations and see how they show up in difficult interactions and relationships.

Questions for Contemplation

1. Notice how your inner thoughts arise and rule you as if they are "the truth" when they are simply how your mind interprets and assesses information and experiences. Can you talk back to them and play devil's advocate so the thoughts you're having are thoughts you want to have?

2. What is the general direction of your thinking? Is it positive, negative, or neutral?

3. Where did your thinking come from? Is it your mother's, father's, teacher's, or a community's? Does it really belong to you?

4. Pick an issue or concern that is bothering you. Now

apply the FFORR technique to it.

- Find where it bothers you.
- Feel the feeling fully.
- Open and allow it to move.
- Release it through your body.
- Rewire and create the emotion you want to have.

Now what is the experience of that concern?

Light at the End of the Tunnel

Think about a thought you typically have, such as, "I have so much to do today." Much of the time this thought is seen as a precursor to other thoughts, such as, "I'm so overwhelmed," or, "I'll never get everything done," or even, "Why me?" Just notice how the interpretation of a thought can be a downward spiral *or* an opportunity. So for instance, "I have so much to do today," can also be interpreted as, "I am moving more fully into living my purpose," or, "Think of all the people I will be able to support today," or, "These are things I want to be doing," or if not, "How can I move through these quickly (delegate, request, etc.) so I can get to the things I really do want to do?" The idea is to make language and the thinking associated with it work for you instead of you being a slave to it.

Chapter 8

Difficult Interactions with Others

Strategy #6: Change the Conversation

*Your vision will become clear only when
you look into your heart. Who looks outside,
dreams. Who looks inside, awakens.*

—Carl G. Jung

A ugust 4, 2004
*The piece of this that I hadn't quite figured on is how
other people react to or judge this issue. For instance, a
girlfriend's girlfriend noticed I didn't like the perfume she
was wearing and rather than think about how it must be
for me to be in this body, she instead got terribly offended
at how I didn't like her perfume and went on to judge
where I'm living and what smells I might encounter there.*

*As I slowly tested the outside waters of the working
world, a participant in one of my seminars was offended
when asked not to wear perfume or colognes. Had I not
had this experience, perhaps I might have felt that way*

as well. I wouldn't normally need or ask for this from someone;, but given how it impacts me, I've become much bolder at asking for what I need.

At first I felt very timid talking about it, but now there's almost a sense of entitlement. "Yes, I can ask for this." "Yes, I deserve this." The more I ask for what I want, the less I make apologies for who I am. There must be an easier way to learn this lesson.

Explaining vs. Outcome

The other day I found myself in a conversation with someone who had not returned a phone call confirming an appointment we'd had, and consequently I didn't show up. I noticed myself caught in a trap most of us repeat. I asked him, "Why didn't you call me to confirm the appointment after I'd specifically called you and asked you to do so?"

His answer unleashed an entire set of explanations that defended his behavior, didn't really answer my question, and took the conversation nowhere. "Well, I thought you would just show…I didn't think I needed to…I figured we'd talk about it when you got here…"

In that moment I realized the question that I had asked had gotten me the answer I was getting. I had asked an explanation question when what I really wanted was an outcome. Questions that start with, "Why didn't you, What's your problem, How come you did it that way…?" all produce a sense of the person needing to defend himself or herself, which can actually block you getting what you really want—a solution or answer to your issue.

In this case I then redirected the conversation and asked, "When can we reschedule?" At this point all I really wanted was an outcome of rescheduling, and we could talk about what went wrong when we met so that we could make sure it didn't happen again. Going into a conversation of explanation only takes the conversation into a negative spiral that is hard to get out of on both sides. And negativity tends to breed more negativity.

Here are some other negative things we sometimes find ourselves saying to others, which take us places we don't want to go:

- "I can't work with you. You're impossible."

- "I knew you'd react that way. You always do."

- "I don't know why I expected anything better from you. You'll never change."

Declarations like these determine the future of a relationship. They leave no room for maneuvering on the part of the receiver. If you tell someone you can't work with them because they're impossible, that's not likely to engender a feeling of goodwill on their part. Instead of wanting to find a way to work with you, they'll feel resentment toward you and may try to find ways to undermine your work. When we make statements like this, there's no good possibility for the future. Instead, it's better to declare how you are feeling rather than how someone else is:

- "I'm so frustrated right now. I need a break."

- "I had a feeling about this. It upsets me too much to move forward in this moment."

- "I'm seeing a pattern that's really triggering me. We need to talk about it, or it will be difficult for me to continue."

- "I'm seeing a pattern that's really triggering me. I need some time to get myself out of it, or I won't be able to have the conversation I'd like to have."

In each of these circumstances the person is declaring what is so for him/her, and in the process releasing the feeling, all the while keeping the door cracked for possibilities in the future. Most people dance around their feelings, having them come out in passive/aggressive moves with other people, or just burning up inside themselves. Many don't even realize what they are feeling.

If you stop and ask yourself, "What am I feeling?" that simple question moves you into a state of awareness, of presence, and prepares you to answer, "Why does this bother me so much?" From there you can do some self-examination and possibly no longer feel triggered. Without it, you are constantly the victim of someone else's behaviors. What do you know?

One of the great inspirational speakers of our time has said that the questions you ask yourself determine your destiny. Think about it. If you were to write down everything you say to yourself, every reaction you have to situations, positive and negative, every moment of sadness, and every happy occasion for a whole week, what would be the underlying questions you were asking yourself? How many times would you ask yourself a variation of these questions?

- "Why am I such an idiot?"
- "Why do I let people take advantage of me?"
- "Why can't I be like so-and-so?"

Your answers to questions like these determine your self-image, and your self-image determines your actions, and your actions determine your destiny. What if we changed the questions we asked ourselves and ultimately our destiny? It's that simple.

Stuart Heller, coauthor with David Surrenda, of *Retooling on the Run*, says that all of us are bureaucracies of habits, that each of us is a whole system of unconscious, repetitive actions. You want to make sure that your bureaucracy is working *for* you, not against you.

The Unaware Piece

Is about how others perceive us in our awareness, and how we may not be aware of it—the unaware piece of our consciousness. Part of the process of being aware is that you come up against someone else's reality. If you perceive that other reality as a brick wall, then you'll only see yourself going around it or bumping against it, trying to tear it down. But if you perceive that other reality as a diaphanous mass, then you can see yourself going through it, with the other person's reality entering into you as a possibility.

Remapping Conversations with Others

Not too long ago I lost it with a friend. We were sitting in a restaurant. I was going through a difficult time in a relationship. I knew it was going nowhere and yet I hadn't garnered the emotional energy to face the fact and do something about it.

My friend thought she was helping by telling me what I was doing wrong and how I could fix it. She thought she was giving me her support, but she was actually giving me her opinion. And lots of it. I couldn't get a word in edgewise. After several tries, I finally screamed, "Would you shut up!"

Needless to say, we had some relationship mending of our own to do after that. All the while we'd been talking, my internal conversation of, "She's not getting it" was building. Because I didn't say anything earlier, it looked like I was overreacting by the time I spoke, but I was just trying to be heard.

In a situation like this one, you may not even be aware of the step-by-step conversation you're having with yourself leading up to losing your temper; but if you walk yourself through it afterward, you'll see how the frustration builds. And it builds through language.

Try this exercise: Think about an incident where you

were upset or lost your temper. Now, go through these language steps.

- I am upset because…

- I first became upset when…

- This reminds me of…

- What I need is…

- What I plan on doing about it is…

Walk back through the incident to find where the hair-trigger reaction came from. For example, you're driving home from a long, hard day at work, and someone slices in your lane in front of you.

- I am upset because this person just cut me off.

- I first became aware of this feeling when I saw how bad traffic was.

- This reminds me of how my boss totally dismisses my suggestions and shows me no respect. My boss cuts me off in conversation constantly.

- This also reminds me of how my father cut me off and dismissed me.

- What I need is to be seen.

- What I can do is ask for that. The next time my boss goes to cut me off, I will ask him to hold his thought rather than trample mine.

The next question is: Why am I so upset about this, really? The immediate answer may be that you have so many things to do, your child is waiting to be picked up, and your partner expects you to be somewhere in thirty minutes. But, of course, if you really think about it, you'll realize the reason you're so upset is because this seemingly casual incident is reflective of your life, or the way you see your life. If you feel put upon or treated unfairly—"I'm not asserting myself enough and my boss and other people are taking advantage of that"—then you'll react very strongly at the slightest thing. That's human nature.

Expressing yourself *to* yourself may not change the immediate situation, but it will likely prevent you from exploding, and it may begin an inner dialogue that can evolve into an outer dialogue with the person or people around you who cause your frustration.

Walk yourself through your feelings about that person with this inner conversation:

- What I assess about this person or situation is…

- I feel that way for this reason…

- What I see myself doing about this is…

- If I were to see the world through his or her eyes…

When you lead yourself to greater awareness with the right questions, it will help you hold scenarios, feelings, and, ultimately, actions in front of you as options, rather than feel victimized by others and the feelings they elicit. This is the ultimate power.

Choosing Words

Words drive the conversation forward, pull it back, or derail it. The more you design your conversations for self-expression and honesty, the more powerful you will be in your life. If you're talking to your coworker and you want to let him/her know that you're getting fed up with a situation, you'll probably say something like, "I'm so angry with you because…" What does this do? It immediately puts the other person on the defensive. You're angry with the individual—not with his or her action. That's what you're saying.

Better to substitute "frustrated" for "angry" and make it clear that it's the situation, not them, that's the object of your feeling. "I'm frustrated about this problem we seem to be having" brings the other person into the equation. From that, he or she is not on the opposite side; he's involved with you in this frustration. You need to engage the other person rather than attack him. Using *we* instead of *you*, as I'm sure you've already discovered, is inviting and pulls someone in on the concern, rather than pushing him into a corner where he has to defend himself. Often when we argue, we want someone to move toward us, but they are so baffled, intimidated, or overwhelmed by the emotion or situation that the other person withdraws and doesn't engage. We end up getting the exact opposite of what we want. Sometimes we do things out of reaction. For instance, answering a question with a question. Someone asks, "Why did you do that?" You answer,

"Why do you think I did that?" It aggravates the situation, and both parties in it, to the point where moving the conversation forward becomes really challenging.

Never answer a question with a question when you're in a conversation with someone with whom you don't have a relationship. This got one of my police clients in big trouble. The officer was writing a ticket on a car and a woman walked up and asked, "Are you writing a ticket for that car?"

His response was, "Does it look like I'm writing a ticket for that car?" She was triggered by his response and reported him for being "belligerent" even though it was really mild sarcasm. As a result, he was reprimanded because her accusation held more weight than his defense.

When this kind of interaction happens, you get further from the point and more caught up in competing with the other person to see who has the cleverest response. In order to get more of what we want, we have to be aware of potential triggers that we could ignite and that will ultimately work against us.

All Conversations Are with Myself

Ultimately, the outer conversations, important as they are for our relationships, will not be successful unless our inner conversations are also cleaned up. Besides defining who we are, our inner conversations define our relationships with other people. Susan Scott puts it very simply in her book, *Fierce Conversations: Achieving*

Success in Work and in Life One Conversation at a Time: "Why is it so important to spend time conversing with ourselves? Because all conversations are with myself, and sometimes they involve other people." The more we are aware of this, the more we can shape those "other people" conversations to work for us.

August 22, 2004

Today was a difficult day. After my housemate exposed me to an extreme amount of hair product last night, I ended up spending the night in the car. Even though I slept pretty well, the ordeal knocked me off balance today. It was one of those days where everything triggered me, with the chemicals making their way into my tissues, liver, and other organs. A day where neurotoxins invaded and I succumbed to their wrath.

I find myself questioning experiences I've had, wondering if they ever really happened or if I fabricated them. I'm also noticing how meaning means more and how hard it seems to get as we interact more but connect less in our fast unrelenting pace that spins us in its own direction.

The balance between being out there in the world with "them" and connecting with loved ones seems to continue to be a challenge for those of us seeking that delicate balance that continues to elude us day in and out.

How can we get the right tip, read the right book, the right piece of advice that will steer us in the right direction with the right person? It seems we need so many right happenings at the right time to achieve something (happiness, balance, enlightenment) that will take us somewhere and then we will be "there."

I'm not sure if we're running toward or away from something, but we move sometimes for the sake of purpose, sometimes for the sake of movement. The stiller I've become, the more I notice how much people move. I often feel like I'm gaining more by doing nothing than if I was out there moving with them. Is that possible?

A friend of mine is a freelance writer specializing in PR copy. Elaine is also a docent at a local botanical garden, where, from time to time, she's contributed ideas for fundraising projects. On these occasions she worked closely with the director of development, a woman with whom she became friendly.

When this woman died suddenly of a heart attack, Elaine was asked by the executive director to write the woman's obituary for the local newspapers. Needing basic biographical information, Elaine stopped by the garden's offices the next day and approached Jake, the media director.

When she explained why she was there, Jake flew into a rage that began with, "Who the hell do you think you are?" and escalated. Elaine listened for about two minutes of this and then shouted back, "Fine, forget it," and left. She contacted the executive director when she got home and asked her if she would email a bio, never mentioning Jake's outburst.

What was going on here? Obviously, Jake was feeling bypassed by the executive director and took it out on Elaine. But his "conversation" with Elaine was really all about himself; Elaine just happened to be in the way. He was really asking himself, "Who am I around here if the executive director can go to someone else to do my job without even mentioning it to me? What does that tell me about my standing in the organization? What does that tell me about how I relate or don't relate to the executive director?" The negative responses he received triggered his anger and Elaine was the receptacle.

Healing and Connecting

I have no way of knowing whether Jake ever confronted his boss, but I doubt it. Most of us prefer to stew. It's easier to keep our anger to ourselves than to confront someone. After all, we have all the control if our anger is internal. We can provide both sides of the conversation. When we internally shout, "Do you have any idea how much you've hurt me?" the person we're shouting at will say, "I didn't until you told me. My eyes are open now and I see how terrible I've been. I can only be thankful that you cared enough to point out the error of my ways, and I hope you'll let me make it up to you." Chances are it won't go exactly that way in real life.

In my book, *Since Strangling Isn't an Option*, I talk about the problem of storing our "dirty laundry"—our anger—rather than airing it. Elaine became Jake's human laundry basket because he refused to deal with whatever problems he was having at work.

What do we lose when we use someone else as a human laundry basket? Well, we could lose our health. We know anger is a strong emotion and we know that negative emotions can have a negative effect on our bodies. A common element among those who suffer pain, whether literal or metaphoric, is a lack of expressing what they need.

In keeping silent, we also lose the ability to connect with the object of our anger in a positive way. We lose the chance to heal—heal ourselves and possibly the relationship.

There are some people who are always going to drive you crazy and some who you will find irritating no matter what you do. But you can learn to live with it if you know that you've explored the relationship openly and fully and resolved to try to bother each other as little as possible. As Scott says, "The conversation is not about the relationship. The conversation is the relationship."

Where do you start? Sometimes it's a simple matter of suggesting lunch. "Do you have time to have lunch together one day this week? I feel as if we haven't been connecting very well lately and I'm concerned about that. I value your input with our work and I'd like us to be able to communicate with each other."

If difficulties have already reached a point where this kind of casual opening is impossible, then ask your supervisor to bring the two of you together to have the conversation, assuming it's in the workplace. It's a good bet if two people in an office are sparring partners, the supervisor will have noticed already and will welcome one of you, admitting there's a problem and asking for help with a solution.

Bring some internal guidelines with you to the conversation. You may want to use any of the several techniques I suggest in, *Since Strangling Isn't an Option...* (For articles and more reading on this go to my website: www.sandracrowe.com.) You may also want to think about what Matthew Budd, coauthor with Larry Rothstein of, *You Are What You Say*, calls his "five linguistic vitamins for health and well-being:

- Make clear requests.
- Decline with respect and dignity.
- Listen to assessments as evaluations, not as truths.
- Convert complaints to clear requests.
- Promise soundly and take care of broken promises.

Using language in these clear and honorable ways keeps the conversation clean and the relationship trustworthy. Have you taken your linguistic vitamin today?

I'll give you an example of a healing conversation. Last year I was called in as a mediator in a lawsuit brought by an employee against his company. Larry was suing because he felt he had been physically and mentally abused by his fellow employees and that this behavior was tolerated by their supervisor.

Larry was from another culture. When other employees teased and clowned around with him on their breaks, he took their behavior as an insult. When he complained to his supervisor, the supervisor shrugged it off, telling Larry they were just having fun and he should loosen up. When Larry couldn't stand it anymore, he hired an attorney and sued.

What was being said and what was being heard? When Larry went to his supervisor, his request was unclear. He thought he was saying, "I'm very unhappy with the way I'm being treated by the other guys. I don't understand why they treat me that way. You're the boss, so I'm asking you to make them stop."

His supervisor heard, "I don't like the way the other guys treat me. They laugh, but I don't think it's funny. I'm not strong enough to make them stop. What can you do about it?"

In response, his supervisor said, "What are you complaining about? They're just having some fun. That's the way guys clown around in this country. Get used to it. It's no big deal."

Larry heard, "You're not one of us or you wouldn't be complaining about this. That's the way guys clown around in this country. If you don't like it, too bad."

Assessments were heard as truths. Requests were unclear. Complaints were left hanging.

By the time I was brought into the situation, it had escalated to a legal dispute and there were hard feelings on both sides. I started by encouraging Larry to unearth all his complaints, giving him a chance to vent. Then I listened to the other parties involved and made some assessments.

This situation wasn't just between two people who were misunderstanding each other. It had affected the entire team. With that in mind, I led the team through a session on personality—how we're different and why and how these differences can influence our work and our attitudes in the workplace.

As a result of this session and our talking, the team's inner conversations were changed, and that change precipitated a change in their outer conversations with each other, which became more open. Once this openness had become their reality, we were able to talk about boundaries, and the team members themselves were able to decide what those boundaries would be.

There's what they do and there's how you interpret it, and they're not necessarily related.

A few weeks ago I forgot my wallet when going to see a new coaching client for lunch. Admittedly, this was not the most professional act in the world, but there I was without my wallet when the check came. I apologized and asked if she would be willing to pay and I would reciprocate next time.

She agreed, but unbeknownst to me I'd pushed a major button in her, so much so that when she got back to the office she began to broadcast how unprofessional this was. It got back to the supervisor of the coaching program, with new twists on it, and boom, I was not only fired from the coaching relationship with her, but was also banned from ever coaching another participant again anywhere in the program. I thought the reaction a bit strong, so I wrote a letter to the head of the program, apologizing and sending testimonials from others I'd coached, which extolled my coaching virtues. That didn't work. I was told never to contact them again, all for forgetting my wallet.

There's what you do and there's how they interpret it. My client spoke of money issues in the session and I'm sure that her having to pay for my lunch pushed some very deep issues that she didn't want to look at and therefore took it out on me. The supervisory staff was all horrified and not one person asked for my explanation or even called to discuss it. They had already decided what happened, what it meant about me, and what they were going to do about it. When someone gets triggered, it is often out of proportion to the thing done, because the trigger is activating an old wound.

Usually the issue gets imbedded and people will act from that issue as a centerpiece of their behavior and values. For example, I know a woman, Donna, who goes out with groups of friends for dinner. She's sociable, outgoing, and a real pain when the check comes. When it arrives she goes through each item and makes sure that every person is responsible for each penny that is counted and that no one pays too much or too little.

On the outside, it looks like Donna is a penny pincher, not wanting to pay more than her fair share, but on closer examination, the real issue is that she wants fairness as a principle to reign at the table, and money is the means for how that should happen. The woman is about fairness more than frugality. She works for a lawyer, volunteers for environmental justice, and talks about equality in all environments. She looks and acts through the lens of fairness, so when she counts pennies (what she does) and drives everyone crazy (how they interpret), nobody really understands why, and they roll their eyes in frustration. Now nobody invites her out anymore.

So when you are the person feeling triggered, here are some questions you can ask yourself to help unpack the trigger:

1. Why does this bother me so much (what's the issue behind it)?

2. What is it reminding me of?

3. How can I let this move through me?

4. What requests and conversation can I have to close the loop on this? Sometimes you will not always be able to talk to the person directly and may need to either speak to another friend about it, a therapist, or simply record it in a journal.

Here's how one friend applied these questions with Donna.

1. To herself she said, "It bothers me because it felt like she was being thoughtless about how I wanted to deal with the check. The issue for me was thoughtlessness."

2. She reflected, "It reminded me of times when family members did not take my feelings into consideration."

3. She acted. "This morning I sat in meditation, felt into my heart, and brought in the *ahhh* sound to open the heart. I began to feel the connection to others in the world. I started with my neighbors, went to others in the neighborhood, and then out to the world. I connected my heart with estranged friends and felt a bonding with many hearts in many places."

4. She took it into the relationship. "Then I called my friend and told her how the situation brought up old feelings of thoughtlessness, and though her intentions may not have been to do so, it was how I felt. She appreciated the honesty and because the conversation was heartfelt and not laced with anger, she took it in and said she would never do it again. The conversation deepened our relationship and my learning of triggers and human dynamics."

So you've got Donna with her issue of equality and someone else with her issue of thoughtlessness bumping up against each other. Without a conversation about this, most people will get angry at the other person for not "getting it"; they will act huffy and potentially end the relationship without ever discussing anything with any awareness. These questions give you fodder for self-awareness, contemplation, and the ability to open the conversation at another level and take the relationship to a new place.

Nonverbal Conversations

When we enter a conversation with another person, what are we looking for? We really want communication, understanding, and a feeling that we're connecting with another human being. In a working situation, add to these a way of building a team mentality, a need to feel we can depend on the other person and let them know they can depend on us, and a way of communicating how we see the other person.

Remember, when we speak, we're not conveying *the* reality, we're conveying *our* reality. The way we see the world is filtered through our past experiences, positive and negative, and through our own needs. When we speak, that filtered reality is what we are trying to express. What others hear is filtered through their past experiences, positive and negative, and their own needs.

We also communicate nonverbally, of course, and our nonverbal communications can be called conversations, too. When a woman nurses a baby, mother and child stare into each other's eyes. Psychologists tell us this is a very important element in a child's bonding, not only with the parent but also with the world. No words are spoken, but the child understands on the most basic level that there's a place for her or him in this new world, and that he or she can feel safe here.

Body Talk

Unspoken communication can also be negative. If you tense up every time a coworker approaches you, he or she will notice your clenched jaw and tight shoulders. What kind of conversation will follow that beginning? A nonproductive one. Richard Strozzi Heckler, author of, *Holding the Center: Sanctuary in a Time of Confusion*, says, "The body doesn't lie." When you're in a conversation with someone, the one constant for both of you is your body language. Even when your lips aren't flapping, your body is talking.

I had a friend a few years ago who decided she wanted to try online dating. But Martie had a problem with only seeing face-shots of the men she was considering. As she says, "I don't know a guy till I see his walk."

You probably know what she means. If a man is walking toward you with his shoulders slumped and his head down, what's your impression of him? That he has the weight of the world on those shoulders? That he has a poor self-image? That he needs a loving mother more than he needs a loving partner?

We all move from a particular part of our body. Those whose orientation to life is more cerebral than instinctive or emotional tend to walk from the head, with their heads out in front of their trunks and arms. Those who move from the pelvis may have a strongly sexual orientation to life. And then there are those who move from the knees— mostly teenagers, who love to strut. How you are in your body is a slice of how you are in life.

An Astute Observer

When you're dealing with a difficult person, it's vital that you observe the person's body language. This will tell you as much if not more about his or her intentions and true feelings toward you, more than the words spoken.

Is this person jittery or rigid? Too familiar (putting hands on your shoulder) or too guarded (standing further away than necessary)? Being an astute observer can be especially helpful when you're in any kind of negotiation or when you're having a conversation with someone you're trying to connect with.

Sometimes we can be so caught up in the moment that our powers of observation get cloudy. At one of my seminars, a woman told us about going to a bar with some friends to unwind after work and meeting a very attractive man. Her friends moved to a table across the room to give her and this guy some private space. "I was so caught up in his charm, I wasn't noticing what they were noticing— that he was a little too comfortable at the bar, as if he spent a whole lot of time there." The woman went on to say that it soon became obvious he was enjoying drinking more than he was her company, and she left him to join her friends. "If you had said to me back then that my friends were picking up on his body language, I wouldn't have known what you were talking about. But now I do. That's exactly what was happening, and I missed it."

Breathing is also a signal in a conversation. It may feel as if there is a lot to keep track of in one conversation, but after a while it becomes second nature. People react through their breathing. When you're saying pleasant or complimentary things to someone, the person's breathing is calm and measured. If you say something angry or threatening, the person's breath becomes quick and shallow. The person may "catch his or her breath" or become "short of breath."

When we're upset or sad, what do we do? We sigh. When we're worried or tense, what do we do? Hold our body rigid and take shallow breaths.

The practice of yoga focuses on breathing because breath is the fuel of life. How we breathe determines how we function physically, mentally, and emotionally. And how we're breathing during a conversation is a tipoff to the other person as to what we're thinking and feeling.

Conversations of Banality

There's a scene in the movie *Forget Paris* where Debra Winger and Billy Crystal are driving with his grandfather in the backseat. The two of them are talking about something that doesn't include the grandfather, so after a while he begins reading aloud all the billboard signs— every irritating advertisement they pass on the road. It's driving them crazy but what they don't realize is that this is his way of participating in the conversation. The problem is he's really not saying anything, and there's nothing the two of them can say to him in response, no way for them to connect, which means the conversation can't move forward.

What the grandfather is really doing in this scene is talking to himself out loud. We all do this sometimes, and I don't mean when we're by ourselves. I mean we've all had conversations in which we're both talking to ourselves and think we're talking to the other person. I'll give you an example of something that happened to me a couple of years ago.

A friend called me and said she'd met a guy she thought I might like to go out with. He seemed like an interesting person, and we shared some of the same interests. I avoid blind dates, but this was a good friend and I thought I should at least give her judgment the benefit of the doubt, so I said she could give him my phone number.

Hal called the following Monday; we talked for a while and set a date for the following Sunday. Thursday he called me on his cell phone and, as he was going over some suggestions for what we might do on Sunday, he interrupted himself to tell me things like, "I'm getting on the elevator," and, "I was just saying 'hi' to someone," and every other little thing he was doing as we were talking. TMI—too much information.

This was a little off-putting, but it was Friday's call that really began sending me signals. Friday, Hal called and left me a message that he'd heard the weather forecast for Sunday and it might snow and we needed to create an alternate plan in case it did. I was busy most of Friday and didn't get back to him. He called me very early Saturday morning, very concerned that our alternate plan hadn't yet been worked out.

At this point, I realized we weren't compatible, and said, "Hal, I'm sorry but I'm going to cancel our date. I think our styles aren't matching up. You seem very concerned with details decided in advance, and I'm a bit more of a spontaneous kind of person."

His response was, "Are you breaking up with me?"

Since we hadn't even been on a date yet, I thought his phrasing a little strange; but I just wanted to get this over with, so I said, "Yes, I am."

And he said, "I think we can work this out in therapy."

Now I was peeved. Therapy? We hadn't even laid eyes on each other! I said, "Okay, I'm getting a little angry now."

Hal said, "If you don't work it out with me, you'll have to work it out with someone else."

I eventually convinced Hal that we weren't going on a date, we weren't going into therapy, and I'd rather work "this" out with somebody else, whatever "this" was.

The piece that made me realize we weren't having real conversations was his Thursday cell phone call, when he proceeded to have what I call a "conversation of banality." I was listening, but I wasn't expected to participate because we weren't having a conversation that mattered. He was telling me every little thing he was doing and there was no place for us to connect and move the conversation forward.

When he called that Saturday, he was having a conversation with himself. Obviously, he'd had this conversation before, so all he had to do was plug in his responses. There was no way for us to connect because we weren't having a conversation. He was. There was no way for the conversation to move forward.

The Sum is Greater than the Parts

When you're talking with someone, do you ever suddenly ask yourself, "Why are we having this conversation?"

What you're really asking is, "What are we creating here? What's going to be the product of this conversation?"

Sometimes the product of a conversation is simply good feelings.

"Hi, how was your vacation?"

"Terrific! We all had a good time."

"I can tell. You look great."

Sometimes the product is a life decision.

"We really think you're the one who can make this work, but it means moving halfway across the country and taking over an operation that's having a lot of problems."

"I know I'm the one who can make this work, and I'm ready to make the changes necessary. Let's do it."

And sometimes the product is a cosmic shift that begins as millions of one-on-one conversations.

"The air we're breathing gets worse every year. There has to be something we can do about that."

"You're right. We need to start seriously thinking about the environment, so that the air our grandchildren breathe will be better than ours."

The most banal conversation is part of a greater whole. Hal's telling me he was getting on the elevator was part of a conversation he was having with himself, and eventually became part of a conversation I had with myself about why he and I weren't a match. The conversation you have with your children about what they did in school today is part of building your whole relationship with them.

Every conversation, every component of body language, every unconscious signal we send to another human being, becomes part of our spiritual fabric and part of theirs. The uselessly negative rends the fabric; the constructive and positive strengthens the fabric.

So, we've talked the talk and addressed our address. We know how feelings impact our bodies and how language impacts relationships.

Let's take the next step. Let's look at the ways in which the confluence of body language and emotion reside in the greater universal grid.

Seven Energy Robbers

Everybody has needs. Sometimes those needs get met; sometimes they don't. When they don't, people find other ways to get them met, and those other ways are usually through other people. This is what leads to what I call the Seven Energy Robbers. These are the ways people violate you on a subtle level. It's typically not illegal and possibly not even unethical. Many people don't even know they are doing it, and you may not either, but you know something doesn't feel right. Here's how they play out:

1. **Wisdom Robbers.** These are the people who think if they know the right thing, have the right piece of knowledge, or get that one stock tip then they will be able to have more money, be eloquent in an arena, or solve some problem that has been plaguing them. They will drill you, ask for lunches, coaching, keep you on the phone, or even corner you at a cocktail party and ask you for a diagnosis of their latest disease. I had a friend who had someone call her on a regular basis and ask for coaching about her business, ask her for new clients, and meet with her to talk about "things," all as a favor. Initially my friend obliged, but then began to feel a bit used and cut off the relationship,

which is ultimately what you must do in that scenario (unless they have something you want and can negotiate the trade). People without boundaries will find themselves either making these requests or even having the requests made of them. What you must watch out for is complying with their requests in your need to be seen as "nice." This is okay to do in the beginning, but you must watch out for the moment you find yourself complaining about them. My friend began complaining to me about it and then I knew her boundary had been violated. Now it was time to redirect the other person to alternative places to get her requests made. The next time the person called she said no to her requests and gave her a few websites to reference.

2. **Space Robbers**. When they're with you, they will often invade your space, get too close, often stare, and either talk about themselves incessantly, or if they engage with you, ask questions that are invasive or too personal. You feel put off, uncomfortable, and often exhausted trying to navigate around their sense of "not getting it." This can happen often in the dating world when someone meets you and thinks you are going to save him or her from himself. The best thing to do is get away; he has no clear inner compass and will want you to navigate for him.

3. **Power Robbers**. These are people who perceive you as powerful either from positional power or because there's something about you that they assess as powerful, such as the way you dress, your "power hair," or perhaps even a "power body" in a gym or physical environment. They seek out the high and mighty, not because they have something to offer, but because they have something to take. As with the others, it's best to find ways out of the conversation with them. If this is done in a social environment, an easy way to redirect them is to introduce them to someone else or to excuse yourself from the conversation. You can thank them for their interest and politely say there is someone else you need to speak with.

4. **Sex Robbers.** This can happen in a work environment or a social one. While I've observed it happening less these days, it still happens. These people use sex as a weapon to "possess" you in some way. They make you think that you are the most alluring person in existence, playing on any insecurity you might have. There is a conquering mentality that accompanies this, and the motive is typically gaining power through seduction. Once their play is complete they will ultimately want nothing to do with you. It can show up immediately or as a cat-and-mouse game, but either way it's a lose-lose situation for you. Get out before it starts.

5. **Time Robbers.** People who just want to be with you much more than you want to be with them. I've had an old friend who would call me up so we could get together and hang out. I was happy to see him once in a while, as our lives no longer really overlapped, but he kept calling more frequently and began to want to see me every week. When I explained that my schedule wouldn't allow it, he became really angry and insisted that we spend more time together. The truth was, he was recently divorced, hated being alone, and was out of other people to babysit him. Finally, he got another friend. His need didn't go away. He just found someone else to fill it.

6. **Money Robbers.** They think you're going to give them money. You are wealthy, or they perceive you as such; they believe that either being in your presence will make them wealthier or that you will see they need cash and hand it over. Sometimes it's indirect: "I'm having a really hard time this month;" or more direct: "Do you think you could give me a little loan?" The problem is if they start to see you as a bank, they will want future withdrawals. This is more challenging with family members who you may feel obligated to and so testing them by loaning a small amount is a possibility. Never give more than you feel comfortable losing.

7. **Victims.** Victims typically look for validation of their victim positioning. "I can't believe he/she did this to me!" might be a phraseology you've heard from this kind of person. These are the blamers, the "I didn't do anything" people. They can make a career out of making others responsible for the things they "haven't done." It becomes a challenging position for you because helping them may put them back on their feet or it may begin a relationship of enabling, where you are the well and they continue to come back to drink. You can test the waters by giving them some help and seeing if that helps them to boost themselves. Sometimes people act as the actual victim, wanting help or seeming debilitated, and sometimes they will act the opposite way and become bullies.

Bullies are almost always victims repositioned. Same coin, different side. So what to do with the victims? Ask them to consider for a moment what their role in the scenario is. If that's something that they won't answer or you don't want to ask, skip to the second and most important question: "Now what do you want to do about it?" That one question forces them to at least think about an action step that will propel them forward out of the scenario. If they reject any possibility or say, "Nothing can be done," then maybe the real question is, "Do you want to engage with them in this way?" If you can't go through them, then how can you go around? If it's a working relationship and you need to work with them, then who else can you enroll for support? What other allies do you have or can you create in the organization to move above, around, or outside this person?

The challenge with Energy Robbers is to not be paranoid that everyone is waiting to take advantage of you in some way, but to simply be aware. When you get that twinge in the pit of your stomach, pay attention to it and do not ignore it. When someone is asking you for something, ask yourself how you will feel if you say yes or no.

Susan Brown, author of, *The Other Side*, says all of us come into this life with a blueprint. This is a basic tenet of several religions—the idea that we live each of our many lives with an individual purpose, that there are things we need to do for our personal evolution and for the evolution of the planet as a whole.

I'm taking for granted that you see everything in your life as a learning experience. If you think of your lifespan as one long opportunity for learning, then everything becomes part of a greater whole. In the next section, we focus on the most intriguing and satisfying part of that greater whole—the spirit/soul/unspoken.

Questions for Contemplation

1. Pay attention to the conversation you're having with yourself. When interacting with a difficult

person, are you letting your emotions rule the way you interact?

2. How can you ask for what you want without letting your emotions take the front seat? In other words, can you feel the emotion but not act from it?

Light at the End of the Tunnel

Oftentimes the thing that triggers us in someone else is closer than your jugular vein. For this, think, or if you like, write down three things that drive you crazy about a difficult person or persons. They might be things like tardiness, rudeness, arrogance, doesn't listen, etc. Now find three things about your parents that irritated you. For instance, they might not have acknowledged your needs, seen you for who you were, or just got you places late all the time. Now think about three things within yourself you don't like. It could be disorganization or you're preoccupied with your stuff or even that you don't focus on *you* enough.

Now look at the overlap between the three. Were there things about your parents' behaviors that irritated you that also showed up in the behaviors of the difficult person? Did you see qualities of the difficult person's behavior that you found within yourself? The more you can identify origins of your "triggered-ness" of other people's behavior, the less it will affect you. The awareness will not only soften the blow, but give you new options in handling things. Now go find that person who triggers you and see if you notice a difference in your reaction to him/her. It may or may not go away, but something should change. Now from here you can go on to make the requests that could permanently change the dynamic. When something in you changes, something in the pattern changes. Welcome to a new pattern!

Chapter 9

Sandpaper for the Soul

Strategy #7: Glean the Lesson

What seems nasty, painful, or evil, can become a source of beauty, joy, and strength, if faced with an open mind. Every moment is a golden one for him who has the vision to recognize it as such.

—Henry Miller

September 4, 2004
What a difference a day makes. Two steps forward, one step back. Got very triggered today smell-wise. Had a reaction to some hairspray someone had on and I was sick for hours.

In a certain way, death would be so much easier. There is a finality to death. You know you are moving toward something in a period of time. With this I aimlessly move forward and then back, never knowing when it will either hit me, or how far it will go in either direction. It's like being lost at sea thinking you're moving toward land, only it turns out to be a mirage.

The good news is that every time I realize it's a mirage, I quickly locate another piece of land to move toward.

On a brighter note, I had some neural depolarization yesterday and I think it's having a very good effect on me. Yesterday I felt it really cleanse the cells of my body and in doing so release a lot of what they were holding onto. Bottom line is I felt more relaxed and I have not experienced any of the nervous tension inside my cells since I've been doing this. The tingling and numbness have diminished as well. At one point these were so pronounced, it woke me up throughout the night.

If I'm looking at the glass half full, this is a reminder of how far I've come. According to my practitioner, I've done in eight or nine months what it takes people three or four years to experience. I can't imagine anything much more frightening than to suffer like this for that long. Please, God, help me to get to the other side.

September 24, 2004

Two days away from the one-year anniversary of all this, and my own freedom is finally in sight. I feel like a baby robin pecking and pecking my way through a hard shell, struggling to emerge, not knowing what's on the other side but pushed to move in that direction.

I finally have the right combination of modalities coming together. While I had some results with bio-set, there were still many missing pieces—continuous exhaustion, not thinking straight, feeling weak, feeling as if I weren't in my body.

Having had my way with that, I've discovered the Computron, but more importantly Jackie, who runs it. The Computron is a meridian-based EDS (electro-dermal screening) machine that assesses every organ and system in the body. Jackie is the woman who operates it. She is an almost naturopath with a heart of gold and years of experience. She finds it and she heals it. But more importantly, she loves you in the process. The day I talked to and met Jackie, my healing began to take place at a deeper level.

Knowing there is finally someone out there who cares, who has true compassion for my ordeal, is somehow opening me up to healing in a way that could never have taken place otherwise. Caring is curing. Finally someone who knew, loved. I'd had other people concerned, but with no capacity to help, causing me to feel thrown out in a dark alley, alone, wet, destitute. There is no greater torture than the torture of fear. There is no greater entrapment or persecution. There is no greater feeling of freedom than when possibility introduces itself.

My experiences with the chemical injury to my nervous system have been life-threatening and life-changing. Out of this terrible ordeal came something so wonderful, so insightful, and so uplifting that it did change my life, and I never saw it coming. My misery was one of the most spiritual experiences of my life.

When I use the word spiritual, I'm referring to that unspoken part of ourselves that is connected to the greater whole, beyond the physical and emotional components of our existence. Some call this spirituality, some call it soul. I've come to think of it as, "A Horse with No Name." Remember the Eagles' song from the '70s? *"I've been through a desert on a horse with no name / It felt good to be out of the rain."* That's what it is to me—an unidentified entity that gets me through the deserts of life, the periods of difficulty and pain.

I prayed during my ordeal. One night I felt I had hit bottom. None of the doctors I'd seen could diagnose what was happening to me. I hadn't worked in months and I was lying in bed, wondering how I could survive if I couldn't breathe.

But even as I was breaking down, crying uncontrollably, and praying, "I just need help," I was realizing I still had much to be thankful for. Even as my body was turning on me, refusing to operate on the most elemental levels, and my thinking was becoming fuzzy and distracted, that "Horse with No Name" inside me could reach out to connect with some sense of hope.

Life is about the mastery of breakdowns, the serious kinds of breakdowns that mire us in pain so deeply it can only be called suffering.

Few of us experiencing that kind of pain would ever think of it as a positive experience. But looking back on it, we often eventually see that there was something beneficial that came from the experience. This is why I think of suffering as a kind of sandpaper for the soul. Just as grits of sand have to irritate the oyster in order to create a luminous pearl, so do our souls need suffering to create our luminosity, our light.

A few years ago I spoke at a World Bank conference in Warsaw, Poland. While there, I met a Rwandan woman, Alayana, who had lost most of her friends and many of her family members in the genocide in the mid-nineties.

Alayana blanked out what happened to her for almost six months; and then, when it came back, it hit her like a meteor, ripping apart her world, plunging her into a desperate kind of pain. And yet, when I met her, she seemed a very well-adjusted person, certainly not someone haunted by tragedy.

She explained to me that she had a very hard time for quite a while and then she said, "I realized that the present moment was what I had. If I brought the past to that moment, then the past would always be my present, and I didn't want to live in that horrible place. I wanted to be here and now, with those loved ones and friends I still had. I forced myself to appreciate what I had and stop mourning what I'd lost."

This is always our choice when we're suffering, isn't it? Live in the past where the pain is, or move through the present into the future. Sometimes, though, we get hung up on the *why* of it all. "Why did this happen to me?" we ask. "I'm a good person. I did nothing to deserve this." We look for logic in the labyrinth of being—some signpost along the path through our misery.

It's one of the oldest puzzles of human existence, why a benevolent divinity allows us to suffer. Many of us spend our lives looking for an answer to that question, reconciling our faith with our losses, hurts, and personal demons. Sometimes the sense of betrayal when terrible things happen to us is overwhelming and we lose our faith. Most of us, though, cling to the assumption that there is a reason—that some good comes from the bad.

There are those who believe that we learn something from suffering, that it's the road we travel to our own evolution into a better person. For those who believe in reincarnation, the suffering we experience is part of the blueprint we worked out for ourselves for our current life, a means of teaching us what we need to know this go-round. For those who believe in a personal God, suffering is a way of drawing us closer to him or her, a means of connecting on the deepest level with our own humanity and through that with the divinity.

Whatever our beliefs, suffering can connect us to a spirituality we may not have experienced before, and connecting with that spirituality can become part of the healing process.

Addressing the Spirit

Earlier we talked about addressing our address—recognizing the bond between our physical selves and our spiritual and emotional components. Now I want to talk about addressing those components as a means of healing.

I had an awakening moment a few years ago. I was

having dinner with some friends, one of whom had brought a friend of hers. This friend of a friend, Dorothy, told us she'd been limping for almost six months but she hadn't done anything about it because she didn't have health insurance. My friends immediately suggested she see a spiritual healer from Brazil with whom they'd worked. Dorothy said she would and we moved on to other things. Afterward, I asked my friends, "Why did you immediately suggest going to the spiritual level?" and with complete certainty they said, "Because when things on the physical level don't resolve themselves, then it's time to move to another one." They assumed, since Dorothy's body hadn't healed itself, that her limp was the result of some spiritual or emotional imbalance.

I was intrigued by this, because I'd been having pain in my shoulder for years. I'd get treatments and the pain would subside for a time, but it always came back. The day after this dinner, I had an appointment with my acupuncturist, and I told her, "I want to work on another plane." We'd been using traditional acupuncture techniques, and these had been helpful on that same temporary basis, but I was ready to try stepping up to the next level.

We started by doing muscle testing using vials holding singular emotions, e.g., sadness, anger, frustration, fear. My body tested positive to the vial containing frustration, which was a signal to my acupuncturist that she needed to balance that aspect of my spiritual plane.

After an hour's treatment, the pain in my shoulder was

completely gone. Not diminished, not feeling better—completely gone, for the first time in years. I felt so incredibly free, I started laughing. And the pain hasn't come back. The memory of that pain, however, has served as a place of connection, a bridge between understanding and compassion.

Experiencing our Humanity Through Others

Once, at a meditation seminar, I found myself seated next to a woman who began to strongly jiggle during meditation. Her jiggling bumped her chair against mine, continuously. It was incredibly annoying, especially during what was supposed to be a quiet time of reflection.

I finally leaned over and touched her very lightly on the arm. No response. The jiggling continued. Once again I leaned over and touched her on the arm. This time she looked at me with a glare of intense anger and dislike, and in a deep whisper that flirted with a scream said, "I can't help it." Then she shot up from her chair and went to sit in a chair against the wall.

When the session was done, she came over to me and said, "I'm sorry. I'm in a lot of pain and I can't control my body when I meditate." I felt such overwhelming sadness for her that I burst into tears.

"I feel your pain" has become an overworked and not very funny punch line, but that's exactly what I was doing with this unfortunate woman. My own experience with chronic pain enabled me to understand what she was going through on a very visceral level. When I told her I was sorry and understood, I was saying it from the depths of my own remembered despair. What started as an altercation became a deep connection. This is true not only in our relationships with people but in our relationships with situations.

The long ordeal that began with my buying a new home has been resolved. I have my life back. But it's a different life because I'm a different person. I am different in relation to myself and different in relation to others.

When it became obvious I couldn't live in my house, I began staying with friends. A few nights here, a few nights there, calling on my friends for support such as I'd never asked of them before.

Some came through like champions, and it deepened our friendship. Some stepped back, and I found our friendship had been a shallow, pleasant thing that I could live without.

Most importantly, though, this experience taught me a lesson about what we give to others and what they give to us. I learned that one of the greatest gifts we can give to others is to need them. No other gift so enriches both the giver and the taker.

June 6, 2004

My favorite day of the year. Today is exactly one year after I bought the house, though I moved in later. So grateful for my condo as a place to turn to, a refuge. After eight months of almost constant shaking, my nervous system is finally coming down. It feels very vulnerable still, but I can do things with ease that were impossible before—go to the grocery store without fear, go to a friend's house without hypervigilance.

My life has become very compact, intimate with itself, and yet on some level very satisfying. I'm able to appreciate it and the things within it, in a way I could not have before. While my life is not the same, I don't think I ever want it to be the same. I have new awareness and appreciation for what I could not have known before. And I am grateful.

Chapter 10

Lesson Revealed:
A Meal for the Beloved

October 15, 2004
The sound of the wind calls me. I want to enter into it, diving into the core of the place where sound originates. I want to disappear there. I want to know how to enter into nothingness and still exist.

In a certain way, this is the most difficult time. My energy is much better, and my desire to get up and move and even be a part of the world is much stronger. Yet I'm restrained by the wall of chemical sensitivity that bars me from entering the world of normalcy.

The day before yesterday I went out to buy some clothes for the first time in almost a year, and after an hour of that I was drained beyond belief. It was as if the everyday chemicals in the air we all take for granted had entered me on a cellular level and had their way.

Emotionally I handle this as part of the comings and goings of my reality. I know when and if I choose to go out I will have a barrage of things to deal with that most people will never know. Yet if I don't engage, I'm filled with excess energy, frustration, loneliness, disconnection, and isolation.

Much of the time, the emotional pain is worse.

I must, as I fight for my healing, do the things physically that will move me forward. I have so far. Cleaned up my gut (lower and small intestine) and regenerated my adrenals. I'm now fervently working on my liver/gallbladder, while I also clean up residual related pain in my right shoulder and upper back.

What that means is that while I'm taking the right supplements, I have to deal with dizziness, nausea, being off balance, out of sync, and out of my body while everything tries to readjust.

It is frustrating and sometimes feels like a losing battle that must be fought. Just because the mountain is high, that doesn't mean it can't be climbed. As long as you can see the top, it's worth it. We get propelled in different ways. Sometimes it's the Concorde and sometimes it's a row boat, but we still get there.

The great poet, Rumi, compares difficult times we experience to chickpeas cooking in a pot. "They keep trying to jump out, and the cook keeps batting them back in with his spoon. Life is cooking us, and we resist because we don't know our purpose in life, the 'meal' that is being prepared."

He says, "Let yourself be transformed into something even better—a meal for the Beloved." If we are able to keep our eye on a higher prize, then the challenging experiences we face begin to take on meaning. If we have meaning, then, as Viktor Frankl says, the suffering ceases to be that.

Throughout this book, we have discussed strategies for dealing with what seems too big to take on, too much to handle, or too overwhelming to comprehend. Here is a review of some of the key concepts that I hope you will keep in your treasure chest.

- Give yourself permission to see the reality of what you're experiencing. Know that you will be able to handle it. Tell yourself, "I'm not given anything I can't handle."

- Stop any mental chatter that doesn't support you. Stand up to your thoughts. Say to yourself, "That thought doesn't work for me."

- Meet the feelings that come your way as guests; invite them in long enough to get to know them, but not so long that they stink. Internally ask yourself, "What am I feeling? Why does this bother me? What does this remind me of?"

- Notice your internal as well as external conversations. See how this shows up in your relationships. Ask people you trust for feedback. "What do you think I could do better?" is an inviting relationship question.

- Look at the learning from what you're dealing with. Sometimes it's hard while you're in something. Ask someone else, "What do you see for me in this?" and later for yourself, "Can I see how I'm different as a result of this?" "How is it shaping me to be a better human?"

As you ask these questions breathe in the words of the poet Rainer Maria Rilke, who so beautifully reminds us to take in, to pull through, and mostly to use what we've been given.

> Quiet friend who has come so far,
> feel how your breathing makes
> more space around you.
> Let this darkness be a bell tower
> and you the bell. And as you ring,
>
> what batters you becomes your strength.
> Move back and forth into the change.
> What is it like, this intensity of pain?
> If the drink is bitter, turn yourself to wine.
> For is not impermanence the very
> fragrance of our days.
>
> —Rainer Maria Rilke

Rise Above to Go Beyond

This morning I woke up in a tizzy with thoughts spinning about something that felt monumental in the moment. I went to mediate for a few minutes before my day began.

As I sat down to remember the highest, I noticed that my concern, as fire red as it had been a few moments prior, somehow shifted in intensity and perspective. By focusing on the Divine, it helped me to remember what *is*—what is important, what is lasting, what is pure, and what is outside of all that we get lost in during our daily lives. *Helicopter Perspective,* as I've mentioned, is what I call it, as it calls us to whirl above the daily musings of life's ebb and flow to see all this in context, to remember the temporary essence of breathing, and to reflect now, with the cognizance of awareness to guide us.

Not only will this perspective give us pause, but it will also give us cause—cause for right action, action that is in alignment with what our soul calls for and perhaps even demands. This is what we must remember; this is what we must hold on to in the brightest of times and in the darkest of moments.

We must hear that voice, no matter how quiet or loud, somewhere in our being, reach out and ask, "Where is the possibility?" We must have *that* question be the guiding one that we keep posing to ourselves and to the highest. We must never let the light of that question dim, for our destiny is contained within it.

We must resolve and commit ourselves to what's possible for us as individuals, to our community, and to our world. Holding ourselves in the space in which that question exists, and holding the light in which we are held, is our mission and our destiny.

Right now, as you read the last few sentences of this passage, consciously connect with the ground below you and the sky above. Feel the gravitational pull that allows no exception and the heavens that have no bounds. See yourself existing in that plane and feel the space around your body open, invite, let in, and welcome the celestial potential that is always present. Know that presence is there for you, assisting you, loving you. Ask what is possible for you in whatever you are dealing with. This opens the door from which another door may be cracked, bolted, or barreled through.

Trust the process. If nothing else, trust the process. Even if you can't see the light, know the tunnel continues. Know there is more. There is so much more.

Questions for Contemplation

1. What have you realized from reading these words?

2. What new actions and reactions are available to you that weren't before?

Light at the End of the Tunnel

See what phrases create new possibilities in your being. Take them as souvenirs or create your own.

- I can move through difficulty with more awareness because I know and trust that even if I don't like it, everything is happening for the best.

- I can take actions that are risky because I know the reward is in the acting, not the outcome.

- I feel the doors of possibilities opening for me and I am moving into what awaits me with inspiration.

- I can rewrite the destiny of my relationships with my awareness and intention, and enjoy their fruit.

Questions for Contemplation

1. How has the awareness you've acquired from your situation shaped you? How are you different?

2. What do you want to learn next?

Appendix

It's September 2011, exactly eight years since this happened to me. It's now a memory, somewhat distant, and in some ways it feels like it never happened to me. Only the moments of smelling the scent of a toxic dryer sheet, or an overly perfumed woman remind me that this ever happened. I carry the scar, but I don't wear it. I don't see through the veils of the lesson; I put them in my back pocket and pull them out as needed. I am forever moved by the experience, but not dictated by it. I am grateful for the places it has taken me—more fullness in what it means to be human, more patience, and more impatience, a larger capacity for love and for fear, and a deeper desire to serve. The feeling of gratitude is deeper in my being, and I look for it in the smallest of events.

I am grateful that you have taken the time to read this and pray that it serves you in some capacity in your life. I hope that it has given you some perspective, a new way of viewing, interpreting, and reacting to your own difficulties whenever or wherever they might be. No, I didn't sign up for this, but like it or not I will take it and I will use every aspect of it for my highest and for yours. Many blessings on your journey.

It has been an honor and a pleasure to be in a relationship with you in this way. Please stay in touch by going to my website and signing up for future updates, articles, and more solutions to everyday relationship and personal dilemmas at: www.sandracrowe.com.

Acknowledgments

No man is an island and no book ever gets written by one person. All the idea makers, shape-shifters, teachers, and contributors mold and fold themselves through the thoughts and lens of the person fortunate enough to have received those teachings. I am no exception to that rule. I have been blessed to sit at the feet of some very wise beings, and your imprint finds itself in the words and in between the lines and thoughts on these pages.

My foundational appreciation starts with my parents, Ethel and Dallas Crowe, who leveled the playing field for me by opening up the world of educational possibility. Without their dedication and encouragement it would have been hard to get out of the gate.

To the many teachers I have encountered, some who have helped me to think differently about the world we find ourselves in, including, and certainly not limited to: Julio Ollia, Richard Heckler, Stuart Heller, Ibrahim Jaffe, Rahim Bronner, James Keeley, Swami Chidvilasanda, Sidi Al Jamal, Richard Dignan, Paul Werder, John Wadude

Laird, Lori Palatnik, Ruth Baars, and many others I have learned from.

For the encouragement and support to see this book through I am eternally grateful to: Kanu Kogod, Krista Kurt, Elaine Cooperman, Harvey Goldberg, Barbara Gluck, Alice Monroney, Robert Hart, Rosie Chavira, John Healey, Laurie Friedman, Stephanie Katz, Alex Knox, Bonnie Patterino, Dean Andrea, Dick Oliver, Venu Sripada, Lydia Vine, Rhonda Gordon, Mike Broadwell, Joelle Norwood, my writing buddy Catherine Morris, and the Women of the Network of Light. You have been my torchbearers, and I feel honored and grateful to have you in my life and in my heart.

Know that I am also in the deepest gratitude to my dearest coaching clients and to the thousands of people who have been in my seminars over the years. I have learned as much if not more from you than I may have taught.

Thank you to all who have contributed in a big way and just as much to those who have contributed in an unseen way. Perhaps the largest unseen way comes from my precious companion, Dulce, a lab mix. While many may say I rescued her, she has in fact rescued me. Her unending love, patience, compassion, and service has taught me more about what it means to be human than anything I may have been able to learn from a human. Thank you, dear one, for saving me every day.

And lastly, I acknowledge the seen and the unseen beings who silently cheer us on, no matter how many times we may stumble or fall. I hear your silent cheers and am screaming in appreciation right back.

I would love to be in touch with you, dear reader. Please go to my website: www.SandraCrowe.com or my Facebook page (Sandra Crowe) to get on my email list. You are wholeheartedly invited to email me at sc@pivpoint.com. While the connection is already there, I look forward to solidifying it. Blessings

About the Author

Sandra Crowe, president of Pivotal Point Training and Consulting and the author of *Since Strangling Isn't an Option...* is a speaker, coach and seminar leader with over 20 years of experience in the communication field. A certified ontological coach with a Masters in Applied Psychology, she speaks and coaches on topics that include "Dealing with Difficult People and Situations", "Staying Calm when the World Around You is in Chaos", "Wellness Management", "Teams that Work", and "Leadership Presence". She consults in Fortune 500 companies such as Marriott, Citicorp, Sony, Southland Corp, and many government agencies as well including The White House, FBI, Social Security, and NASA. She has been written about in *The Washington Post, The New York Times, The Philadelphia Inquirer, The LA Times, Glamour, Redbook, Good Housekeeping, and Men's Health* and featured on TV appearances such as the CBS Morning News, To Tell the Truth and the ABC evening news. She also had her own TV show *StressBusters,* a Washington, DC based program. A contributor to the book *Chicken Soup for the Soul at Work,* her work has also appeared in trade journals and magazines. Her mission is to create awareness of ineffective behaviors and redirect them for more uplifting interactions. Please visit her website to receive emails and updates at www.SandraCrowe.com or email at sc@pivpoint.com. You can find her on FB under Sandra Crowe and on Linked In and Twitter @SandraSpeaks4u.